#2
3/22

CREATIVE CARDS

Kodansha International
Tokyo and New York

CREATIVE CARDS

Wrap a Message with a Personal Touch

Yoshiko Kitagawa

Photography Tadao Yoshida

Distributed in the United States by Kodansha International/USA
Ltd., 114 Fifth Avenue, New York, New York 10011. Published by
Kodansha International Ltd., 2–2 Otowa 1-chome, Bunkyo-ku,
Tokyo 112 and Kodansha International/USA Ltd., 114 Fifth Avenue,
New York, New York 10011. Copyright © in Japan 1987 by Kodansha
International Ltd. All rights reserved. Printed in Japan.

First edition, 1987
Second printing, 1989

Library of Congress Cataloging-in-Publication Data
Kitagawa, Yoshiko.
Creative Cards

1. Greeting cards. I. Title
TT872.K58   1987   745.594   87-45210

LCC 87–45210
ISBN 4-7000-1318-3 (Japan)
ISBN 0-87011-818-8 (U.S.)

CONTENTS

INTRODUCTION

In Japan, the festive New Year holiday is a time to send greetings to friends, family, and business associates. Many people make their own cards, decorating them with a sketch, brushwork, a woodblock print, or a stamped image.

About ten years ago I began to make holiday cards by folding beltlike strips of silver matte paper and Japanese traditional patterned paper. I called them *"obi* cards" after the *obi* (sash) of the kimono. I sent out about a hundred of these cards, with the year and greeting on the front, my name on the back, and a personal message inside.

I have continued to make them every year. *Obi* cards are my own creation, and people tell me they enjoy receiving one because they know immediately who it is from. And that's just what a card should do: convey your sentiments *and* somehow represent you personally. What could be more meaningful? Store-bought items are adequate, but their main virtue is convenience. There is a special feeling of delight in sending a message in a card not only suited to the occasion but carefully chosen and made with your own hands.

The creative cards in this book have been designed for that purpose. They have a natural warmth that their ready-made counterparts cannot match. No "tricks" or special talents are required—you need only cut, combine, and fold a few pieces of paper. The important difference is the thought and care you put into the cards.

The shape, color, and textures of the card appeal to the eye and touch. You can make a personal statement by varying the color, texture, or tone of the paper to suit the occasion and what you wish to say. The thought with which you select the style and materials will go a long way in conveying your unspoken sentiments.

Naturally, the message should be neatly written, but it's more important that it be personal rather than artistic. Write carefully, but don't worry about your handwriting. You can add simple sketches or use alphabet decals.

When you send your card, I suggest you send it without ceremony in an ordinary envelope. Too elaborate an envelope gives a fussy, labored impression. It's better to finish it casually without emphasizing your efforts. A few cards, such as those in the Glossy Moderne section, can be mailed without an envelope, putting a stamp directly on the card. The marks of handling during delivery add an interesting dimension. And, of course, any of the cards can be enclosed with a gift.

These cards resulted from my desire to add warmth to what had become little more than a bothersome ritual. They succeeded for me, and I am sure they will for you.

Yoshiko Kitagawa

GENERAL INFORMATION

The combination of papers in the card you send says almost as much as the written message itself. It is the colors and textures that set the mood and convey your "unspoken" message. Store-bought cards are usually made of stiff paper, but most of the handmade cards in this book call for softer, thinner, and more flexible paper. In order that the finished card be sturdy, two or more layers are used. The layers are not glued together, but held in place with small pieces of double-face adhesive tape (which can be omitted if you are careful about keeping the papers in position, or if you desire a slight slippage of the paper, which lends a nice handmade look to each card).

Try the easiest cards first, perhaps the Kraft or *Obi* Cards, to get the sense and feel of the recommended papers. Ordinary paper and Japanese paper are used in various combinations to achieve distinctive moods and effects. Basically, ordinary paper has a sharp character, while Japanese handmade paper has a softer, more sensitive feel. Because the papers and colors of the card are part of the message, you can keep your written message short.

Last, it goes without saying that the papers given for each card are mere samples of what can be done and are not the final word on the matter. Experiment with other papers, and even other paperlike material, to make cards that say what you want them to.

TIPS

1. You will need double-face tape, a ruler, compass, protractor, a small utility or craft knife, a stylus or wooden paper knife for scoring lines, and metallic-colored markers. A small, home paper cutter is recommended for straight cuts. Scissors are seldom recommended.

2. For ease in folding, scoring the paper first is often recommended. To score, draw along the fold line using a stylus or a wooden paper knife. Use a ruler so your score line is straight.

3. It easier to get a clean fold if you fold along the edge of a ruler. Fold neatly and accurately. It is important to avoid leaving any trace of your mechanical efforts.

4. Before you must cut slits, practice with your utility knife. Ragged slits are not attractive.

5. For cards that are folded in half, you may wish to fold the paper first and then cut it to the specified dimensions.

6. Ordinary paper must be marked carefully and folded accurately the first time. Refolding shows. Paper has a grain, so diagonal folds must be made carefully to avoid distortion. The softer Japanese papers can be folded in any direction, and you can remake folds as well.

7. Glossy and metallic papers show fingerprints, which makes them look dirty. When folding, place tissue, another sheet of paper, or a ruler on top of the paper, and press gently.

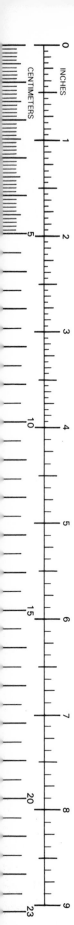

8. Creases can be removed from Japanese paper by putting a piece of cloth over it and pressing with a steam iron. You can do this to "erase" a mistake in folding, or to press the large cards.

9. Practice with scratch paper before you make the card. You can use the practice paper as a pattern.

KEY TO THE DIAGRAMS

Score line ——·——·——·——·——·—— ·—— ·—— ··

Fold line --------------------------------

Direction of fold

Cutting line – – – – – –✂ or ————✂

Double-face tape []

Formal Cards

Congratulations on your wonderful promotion! You deserve it!

*Please Joi[n]
[Bi]ll and Linda
For Cockta[ils]
Saturday, June 1
7 p.m.
7075 Far Hills Drive
RSVP 944-6494*

These elegant cards make ideal invitations to special parties or once-in-a-lifetime celebrations such as silver or golden wedding anniversaries.
(Cards 2 and 3, pages 15–18.)

ThoughtFulls

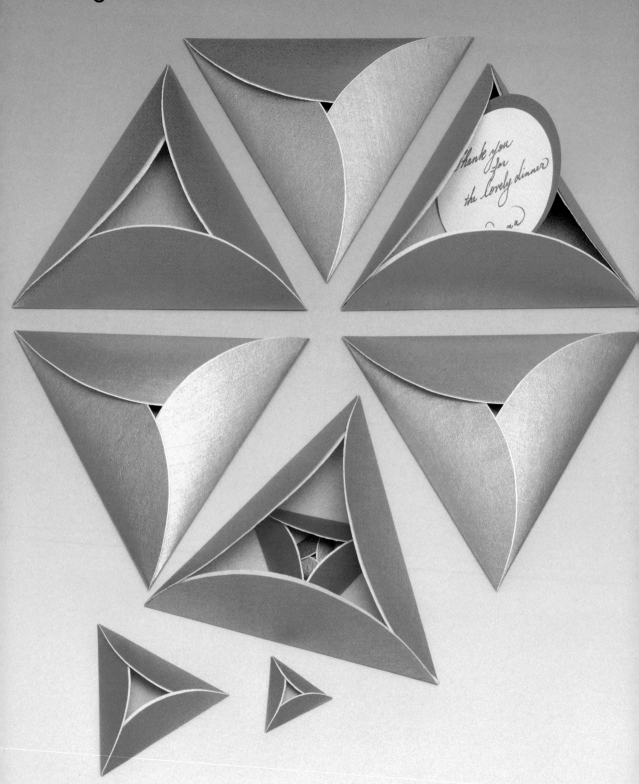

Thank you
for
the lovely dinner

These cards have a refined simplicity. Keep your message brief, and let the card convey your feelings and good taste.

(Card 4, page 19.)

Glossy Moderne

Choose these cards to send your warmest congratulations for the landmarks of life, such as graduation from university, or a first job.

(Cards 5 through 7, pages 21–25.)

Something Natural

Use these cards to send greetings or a message of sympathy to an ill friend. The plant you select should reflect the message and the season.

(Cards 8 through 11, pages 26–32.)

1 Formal Card

Send this card for a twentieth wedding anniversary along with a bottle of fine twenty-year-old wine. The rich, layered effect is revealed as you unfold the card. In typical Japanese style, even the unseen parts are exquisite. Make a shikishi, *the traditional Japanese message card, for your message.*

MATERIALS

1 sheet 13¼ × 13¼-inch orange tissue or *tengujo* paper
1 sheet 12¾ × 12¾-inch gold paper
1 sheet 11½ × 11½-inch red tissue or *tengujo* paper
1 sheet 11½ × 11½-inch silver paper
1 sheet 9½ × 9½-inch brown tissue or *tengujo* paper
wine-colored cord
1 5 × 6¼-inch *shikishi* (see next page)

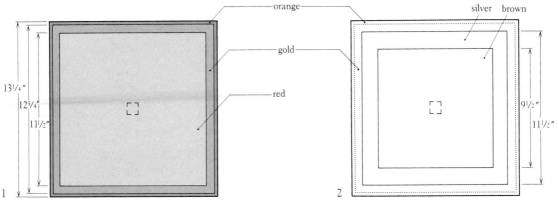

1 Center gold paper on top of orange paper, and fix in place with a small piece of double-face tape in the middle. Center red paper on top of the gold, affixing with another piece of tape just off center to avoid a lump. Turn paper over.

2 Center silver paper on top of orange, and brown on top of that, fixing in place with double-face tape.

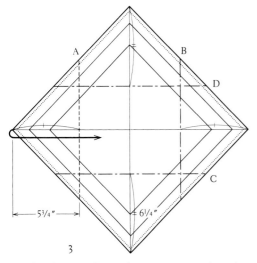

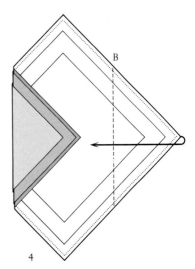

3 Place brown side up, then measure, mark, and score lines A through D. (Note that lines C and D divide the diagonal of the square into three equal parts.) Fold line A, pressing down firmly with a ruler.

4 Fold line B, pressing firmly.

13

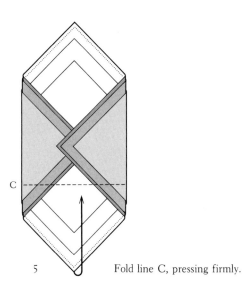

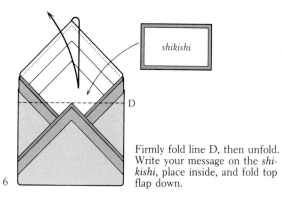

shikishi

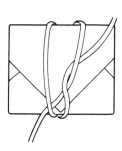

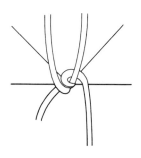

D

C

5　Fold line C, pressing firmly.

6　Firmly fold line D, then unfold. Write your message on the *shikishi*, place inside, and fold top flap down.

7

Wrap cord twice around the card as shown. Pull tight at lower edge of card.

HOW TO MAKE A *SHIKISHI*

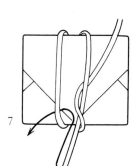

shikishi

color with gold

Cut 1/16-inch-thick illustration board to the specified dimensions, and color a border around the card by running an oil-based opaque gold felt-tip marker along the top edge. Color will spread down the sides and along the surface.

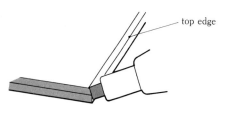

top edge

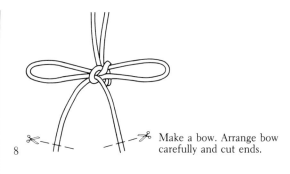

8

Make a bow. Arrange bow carefully and cut ends.

2 Formal Card

Announce special parties with this lavish card. Its layered sumptuousness echoes the twelve-layered ceremonial robes worn by Japanese court ladies in ancient times. The soft tengujo *paper on silver suggests nobility and grace.*

MATERIALS

1 sheet 13 × 13-inch light green tissue or *tengujo* paper

1 sheet 12½ × 12½-inch silver paper

1 sheet 11½ × 11½-inch gray tissue or *tengujo* paper

1 sheet 10⅝ × 10⅝-inch pale orange tissue or *tengujo* paper

1 sheet 10 × 10-inch pale pink tissue or *tengujo* paper

gold cord

1 5 × 6¼-inch *shikishi* (see page 14)

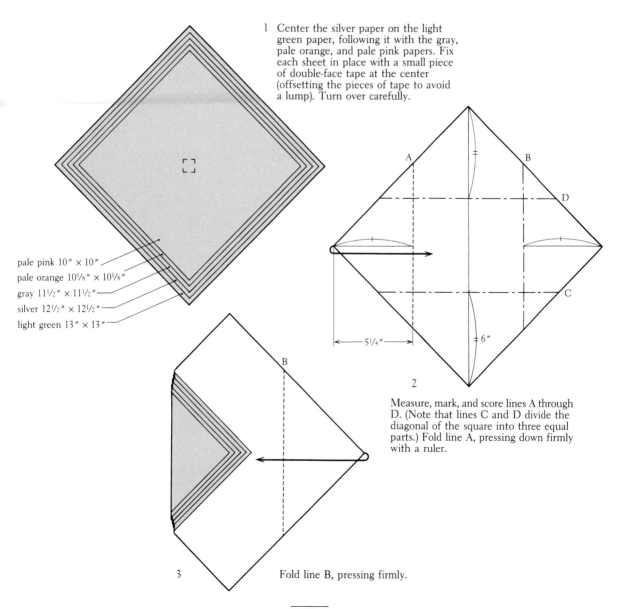

1 Center the silver paper on the light green paper, following it with the gray, pale orange, and pale pink papers. Fix each sheet in place with a small piece of double-face tape at the center (offsetting the pieces of tape to avoid a lump). Turn over carefully.

pale pink 10″ × 10″
pale orange 10⅝″ × 10⅝″
gray 11½″ × 11½″
silver 12½″ × 12½″
light green 13″ × 13″

Measure, mark, and score lines A through D. (Note that lines C and D divide the diagonal of the square into three equal parts.) Fold line A, pressing down firmly with a ruler.

Fold line B, pressing firmly.

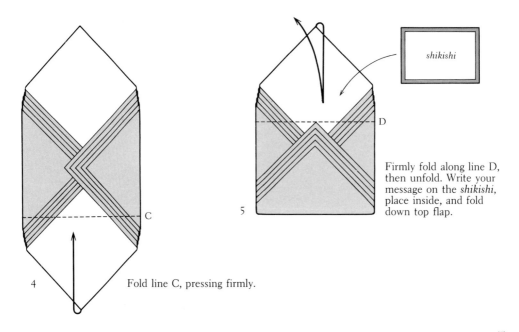

4

Fold line C, pressing firmly.

shikishi

5

Firmly fold along line D, then unfold. Write your message on the *shikishi*, place inside, and fold down top flap.

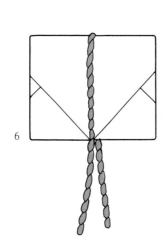

6

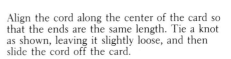

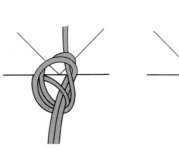

Align the cord along the center of the card so that the ends are the same length. Tie a knot as shown, leaving it slightly loose, and then slide the cord off the card.

Separate the strands of the cord below the knot. To straighten strands, hold ends and moisten with steam from an iron or hot water, tugging at ends until waves disappear. Trim cord ends.

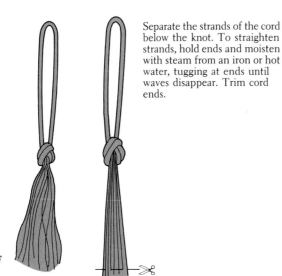

7

8

Slide the cord back onto the card.

3 Formal Card

This card also makes a delightful party invitation. The belted square opens to reveal the original circular shape, an amusing device that anticipates the pleasures of the party. Sturdy Japanese paper makes an ideal belt. Crumple the paper first to make it easier to tie.

MATERIALS

1 sheet 10½ × 10½-inch blue *momigami* or any sturdy textured paper
1 sheet 10½ × 10½-inch gray tissue or *tengujo* paper
1 sheet 10½ × 10½-inch silver paper
2 strips 18 × ⅜-inch gold paper
1 4¼ × 4¼-inch *shikishi* (see page 14)

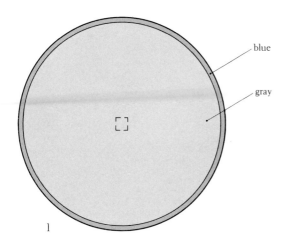

1

Cut a circle 10 inches in diameter from the blue paper, and 9¾ inches in diameter from the gray. Center the gray circle over the blue and fix in place at the center with a small piece of double-face tape. Turn paper over.

2

Cut a circle 9¾ inches in diameter from the silver paper and center it on the back side of the blue paper. Tape in place just off the center to avoid making a lump.

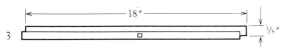

3

To make the belt, place the two strips of gold paper back to back. Fix in place with double-face tape at the center.

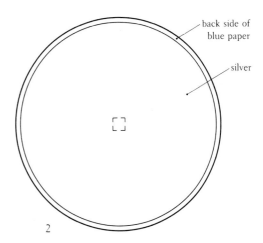

4

With silver side up, measure, mark, and score lines A through D. Fold line A down. Crease firmly, pressing down with a ruler.

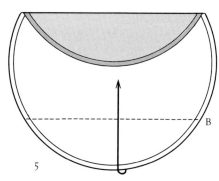

5

Fold line B, pressing firmly.

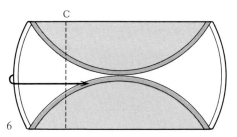

Fold line C, pressing firmly.

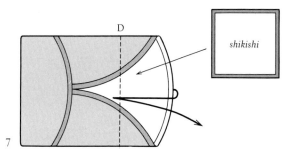

7

Firmly fold along line D. The completed shape should be square. Unfold, write your message on the *shikishi*, and insert.

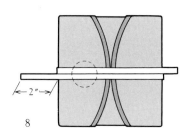

8

Wind the gold belt around the card so that the left end protrudes about 2 inches beyond the card as shown.

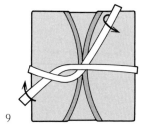

9

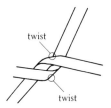

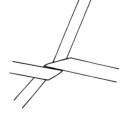

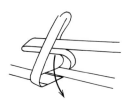

Tie the knot in the circled area (in step 8). Twist both ends of the belt once as shown. Pull tight. Tie the knot as shown, holding the lower knotted part firmly. Pull to remove any slack, shaping the knot carefully as you tighten it. Trim the ends.

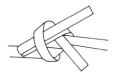

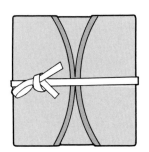

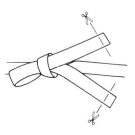

4 ThoughtFulls

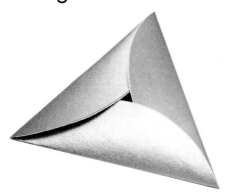

This card offers a geometric twist: inside the triangle is either a circle or a nest of triangles. The bright pastel of the interior appears to float up out of the card when it is opened. The hues used here suggest cherry blossoms, wisteria, and hydrangea, while the message card recalls a crescent moon. You might want to substitute seasonal colors.

MATERIALS

1 piece 8 × 8-inch gold paper
1 piece 8 × 8-inch blue *momigami* or any sturdy
   textured paper
1 circle white paper, 3 inches in diameter
1 circle gold paper, 3¼ inches in diameter

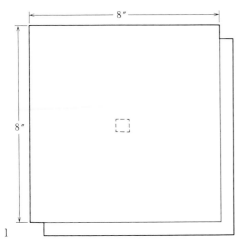

1

Position gold paper and blue paper back to back, aligning corners, and fix in place with a small piece of double-face tape.

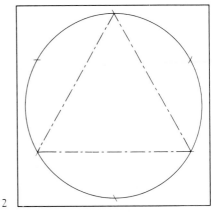

2

With the blue side up, draw a circle 7½ inches in diameter. Divide the circumference of the circle into six parts by setting your compass at the radius length and then marking off six of those lengths around the circumference. Draw an equilateral triangle inside the circle as shown. Score the triangle. Cut out the circle.

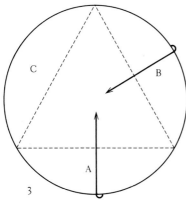

3

Fold flap A up. Fold flap B over A.

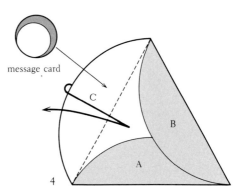

message card

4

Fold flap C, then unfold. Make the message card (see next page).

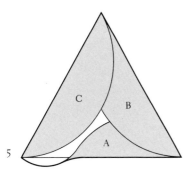

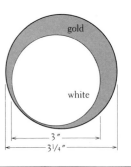

MESSAGE CARD

Attach white circle to gold circle with a small piece of double-face tape, positioning it so that a crescent of gold paper shows at one side. Write your message on the card.

gold

white

3″

3¼″

5

Tuck the edge of C under A.

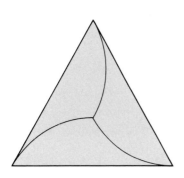

| Variations |

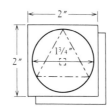

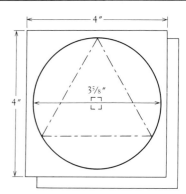

2″

2″

1¾″

4″

4″

3⅝″

Small size
1¾-inch diameter circle

Medium size
3⅝-inch diameter circle

5 Glossy Moderne

The arresting red-on-black is adopted from Japanese lacquerware. The gold belt, like the ware's applied gold flake, adds a special accent. To achieve a look of fullness, make sharp folds at the layered corners but softer, "rounded" creases along the edges.

MATERIALS
1 sheet 10 × 10-inch glossy red paper
1 sheet 10 × 10-inch glossy black paper
1 4 × 4-inch *shikishi* (see page 14)
1 strip 11¼ × 1½-inch gold paper
gold threads

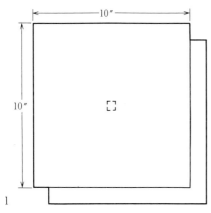

10″

10″

1

Position black paper and red paper back to back, aligning edges, and fix in place with a small piece of double-face tape.

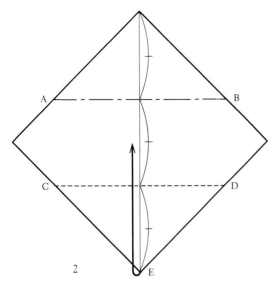

2

With red side up, score lines AB
and CD, dividing the diagonal into
three equal parts. Fold point E up
along line CD.

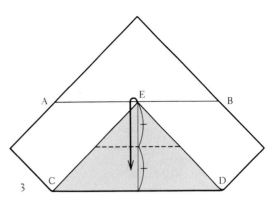

3

Fold point E down to bottom edge,
creasing fold well.

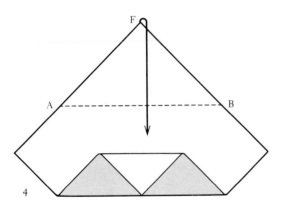

4

Fold point F down along line AB.

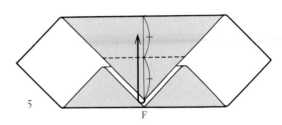

5

Fold point F up to upper edge,
creasing fold well.

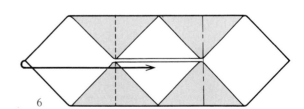

6

Score both lines. Fold left flap in.

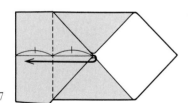

7

Fold the tip back to the left edge,
creasing fold well.

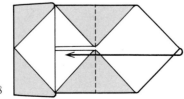

8

Repeat steps 6 and 7 with the right flap.

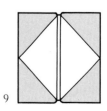

9

Card should look like this.
Insert *shikishi*.

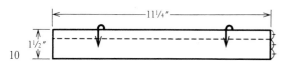

10 Crumple the gold paper and then smooth it out. Place gold side down and fold the upper third down.

11 Fold the lower third up.

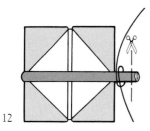

12 Wrap the belt around the card as shown. Wind two or three fine gold threads around ends several times, then knot. Trim belt and thread ends.

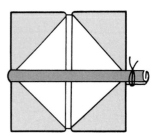

6 Glossy Moderne

The use of gold in tandem with blue or another somber color makes this card appropriate for formal occasions. A shikishi may be inserted or a message may be written directly on the folded paper. The finished piece is impressive even though it calls for only basic origami techniques.

MATERIALS
1 sheet 10 × 10-inch glossy gold paper
1 sheet 10 × 10-inch glossy blue paper
1 4 × 4-inch *shikishi* (see page 14)

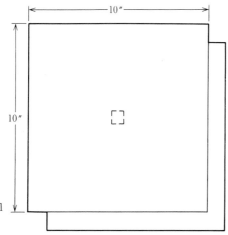

Position papers back to back, aligning edges, and fix in place with a small piece of double-face tape.

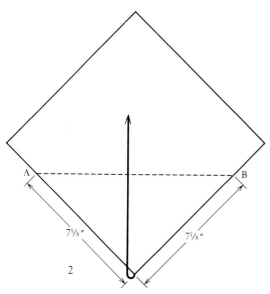

A   B

7⅝″   7⅝″

2

With blue side up, measure and score line AB. Fold lower corner up along the scored line.

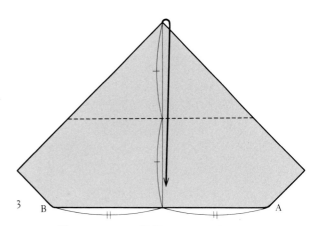

3   B   A

Turn paper over. Fold top corner down to bottom edge. Fold down corner protruding at back, creasing well.

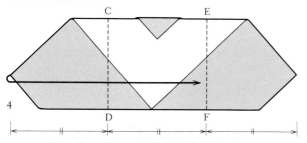

C   E

4

D   F

Score lines CD and EF. Fold the left side flap toward the center along line CD.

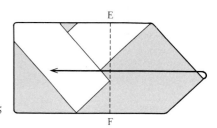

E

5

F

Fold the right flap toward the center along line EF.

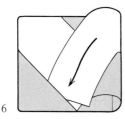

6

Insert the right flap between the layers of the left flap as shown.

7 Glossy Moderne

The contrast here emphasizes the form. And though it looks ordinary enough, as you open the card the intricacy of the layers and folds offers a refreshing surprise. Select color combinations that will appeal to the recipient.

MATERIALS
1 piece 9 × 9-inch glossy yellow paper
1 piece 9 × 9-inch glossy blue paper
1 3¾ × 3¾-inch *shikishi* (see page 14)

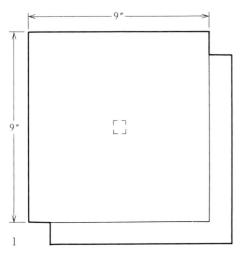

Position papers back to back. Fix in place with a small piece of double-face tape at the center.

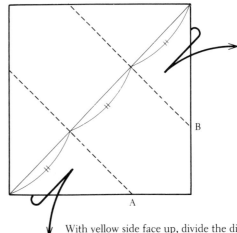

With yellow side face up, divide the diagonal of the square into three equal parts, and mark. Fold at parallel lines A and B as shown. Press firmly to crease. Open paper up again.

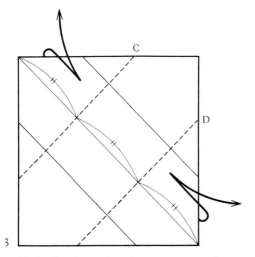

Mark other diagonal in the same manner, then fold lines C and D, creasing firmly. Unfold.

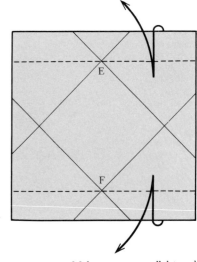

Turn paper over. Make creases parallel to edge along lines that cross points E and F. Unfold.

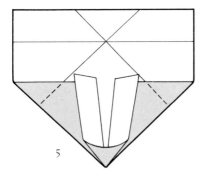

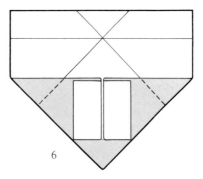

5

6

Turn paper back over. Fold along creases as shown. Press down the tip of the triangle with your finger, making sure the two reverse-side flaps are parallel and meet in the middle.

Paper should look like this. Unfold. Rotate paper and repeat with opposite edge.

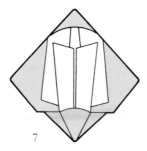

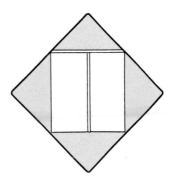

7

Refold first side, then tuck flaps under those made in step 6.

ABOUT JAPANESE PAPER

Unlike ordinary paper, which is made by mechanical and chemical processing of plant fibers from wood pulp or straw, Japanese paper is handmade using bast fiber from the paper mulberry, mitsumata, or ganpi plants, Most paper is made by machine in today's Japan, but the Japanese paper utilized in the cards described in this book is almost all handmade.

In the production of Japanese paper, the plants are steamed, the bark is first stripped then steeped in water, and the skin of the bark is removed. It is then boiled until the fibers become soft, after which it is again soaked in water. The bark is next beaten to form a pulp. Pulp is placed in a vat and mixed with a vegetable mucilage and large amounts of water to form a suspension of fiber particles.

A bamboo screen in a frame is dipped into the liquid in the tank, and tilted and shaken so that a thin layer of fiber covers the screen evenly. This process may be repeated two or three times, depending on the thickness of the paper required.

The fiber—the wet paper sheet—is then removed from the screen and stacked. When a sizeable stack has been formed, it is squeezed with a press to remove most of the water. The sheets are then dried to become the finished paper.

TYPES OF JAPANESE PAPER IN THIS BOOK

Tengujo paper is a thin tissuelike Japanese paper made from the bast fibers of the paper mulberry. Despite its apparent flimsiness, it is strong as well as soft and beautiful. Substitute *unryu* or *usumino* paper, or colored tissue paper.

Chirimengami ("crepe" paper) can be either machine- or handmade. With the handmade type, the crinkled effect is achieved by pressing the paper against the mold by hand or by machine. Substitute any sturdy textured paper.

Momigami is made by crumpling sturdy mulberry paper. This may or may not be backed. Substitute construction paper or any sturdy textured paper.

Chiyogami is a style of brightly decorated paper traditionally made by woodblock printing. This robust style of decoration is associated with the city of Edo (now Tokyo), as compared to the more subdued decorated papers of Kyoto (known as Kyogami). Substitute any medium-weight paper, such as gift wrap.

8 Something Natural

Get out your compass, protractor, and ruler, and you can make some wonderful cards. Slip seasonal leaves or small blossoms between the double layers of thick tracing paper, then wrap the sheets around the message card.

MATERIALS

1 sheet of scratch paper for pattern, about 10 × 10 inches
2 pieces 6 × 6-inch medium-weight tracing paper
something natural—a pressed flower, a leaf, etc.
1 3¾ × 3¾-inch construction paper

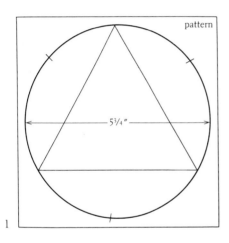

1

Make a pattern first. Draw a circle 5¾ inches in diameter on a scrap of paper. Divide the circumference of the circle into six by setting your compass at the radius length and marking off six points around the circumference. Use three of the points to draw an equilateral triangle. Cut out pattern.

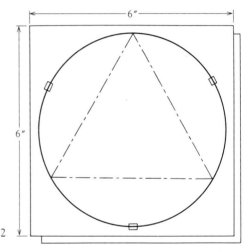

2

Lay the sheets of tracing paper together, aligning the edges. Attach the pattern to the tracing paper with tape. Trace the circular outline and firmly score the triangle. Remove the pattern.

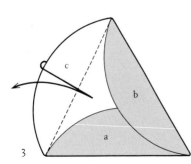

3

Carefully cut out the circle. Fold the flaps along the scored lines in order, B over A and C over B, creasing firmly. Unfold C.

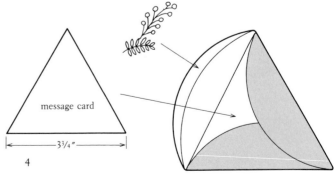

4

Insert the flower or leaf you have chosen between the layers of tracing paper. Cut the message card into a triangle. Write your message on the card and slide it under the flaps.

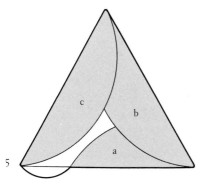

5

Tuck the edge of C under A.

9 Something Natural

These nearly transparent cards provide a glimpse of their contents, enticing the recipient to open them for a closer look, so make the shikishi *for your message particularly elaborate. In this example a white square is used, but you could use any color that complements your flower.*

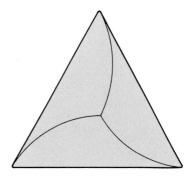

MATERIALS

1 sheet of scratch paper for pattern, about 10 × 10 inches

2 pieces 8½ × 8½-inch medium-weight tracing paper

something natural—a pressed flower, a leaf, etc.

1 3 × 3-inch *shikishi* (see page 14)

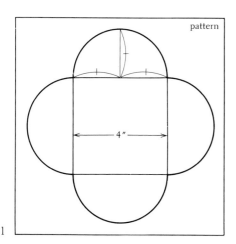

pattern

4"

1

Make a pattern first. Draw a 4 × 4-inch square in the center of a scrap of paper, and draw a half-circle with a 4 inch diameter along each side of the square as shown. Cut out the pattern.

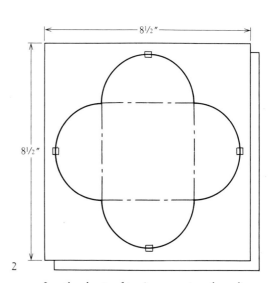

8½"

8½"

2

Lay the sheets of tracing paper together, aligning the edges. Lightly attach the pattern to the tracing paper with tape. Trace the outline. Firmly score the four sides of the square. Remove the pattern.

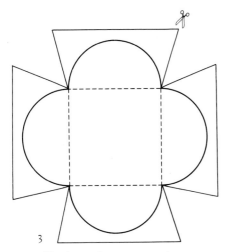

3

Notch out the corners as shown.

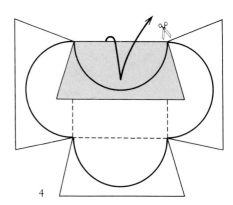

4

Fold and unfold each flap, creasing firmly. Make sure that the two layers stay together. Carefully cut out the shape.

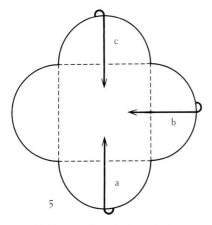

5

Fold down flaps A through C in order.

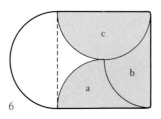

6

Card should look like this.

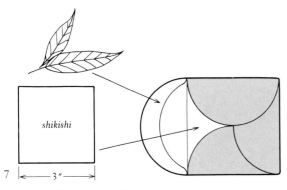

7 |← 3″ →|

Gently insert the flower or leaf you have chosen between the two sheets of tracing paper. Write your message on the *shikishi* and slide it under the flaps.

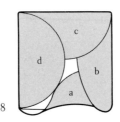

8

Tuck the edge of D under A.

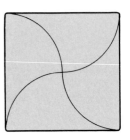

10 Something Natural

The petal-like flaps of this pentagon suit the nature theme. Use a protractor to mark off the angles of the pattern. Once you have made a pattern, the card itself is only a matter of a few moments.

MATERIALS

1 sheet of scratch paper for pattern, about 10 × 10 inches
2 sheets 10 × 10-inch medium-weight tracing paper
something natural—a pressed flower, a leaf, etc.
1 3 × 3-inch *shikishi* (see page 14)

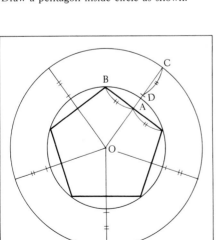

1. Make the pattern first. Draw a circle 5 inches in diameter in the center of the scrap paper. Draw a pentagon inside circle as shown.

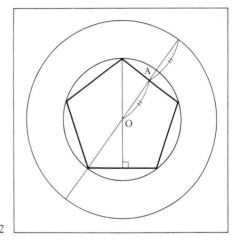

2. Measure the distance from O (center) to A (midpoint on one side of the pentagon). Set your compass at twice this distance, then draw a larger circle around the first, using O as the center.

3. From O, draw lines which bisect each side of the pentagon. Measure the length of line AB and mark off line CD, using the same length. Mark all five lines.

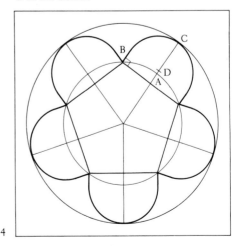

4. Using point D as the center, draw a half-circle whose radius is the same length as AB. Extend the ends of the half-circle to the corners of the pentagon as shown. Repeat for the remaining four sides. Cut out the shape. This is the pattern for the card.

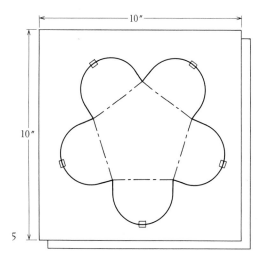

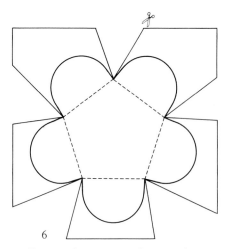

Lay two sheets of tracing paper together, aligning the edges. Affix the pattern to tracing paper with small pieces of tape. Firmly score the overall shape and the pentagon.

6

Remove the pattern and cut notches between the flaps as shown.

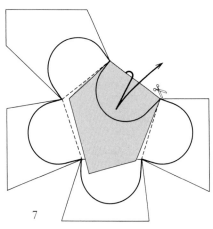

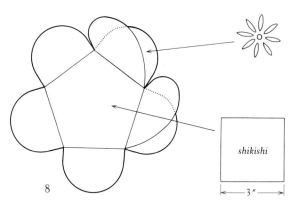

shikishi

— 3″ —

7

Fold one flap inward along the side of the pentagon and crease firmly (being careful that the layers don't separate), then unfold. Repeat with remaining flaps. Cut out the flaps carefully.

8

Gently insert the flower or leaf you have chosen between the layers of tracing paper. Use a square *shikishi* or cut a pentagon slightly smaller than that of the card. Write your message on it, then slide it under the flaps.

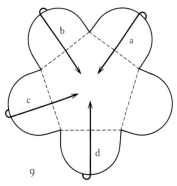

9

Fold down flaps *a* through *d* in order.

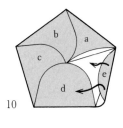

10

Slip the edge of flap *e* under flap *a* as shown.

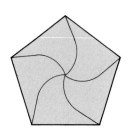

11 Something Natural

This hexagonal card with overlapping flaps must be cut carefully so that the flaps meet exactly in the center for a petal effect.

MATERIALS

1 sheet scratch paper for pattern, about 10 × 10 inches
2 sheets 10 × 10-inch medium-weight tracing paper
something natural—a pressed flower, a leaf, etc.
1 3 × 3-inch *shikishi* (see page 14)

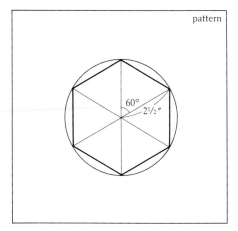

1

Make a pattern first. With a compass, draw a circle 5 inches in diameter. Draw a hexagon inside the circle by marking off the radius measurement six times around the circumference and linking the points with straight lines.

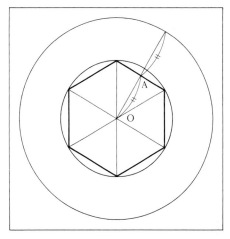

2

Mark the center of one side of the hexagon. Draw line AO. Measure the length of AO, then draw a larger circle with a radius double the length of line AO, as shown.

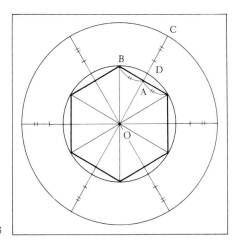

3

From point O, draw lines that bisect each side of the hexagon. Measure the length of AB. Mark off the AB length and, measuring from the outer circle inward, mark line CD.

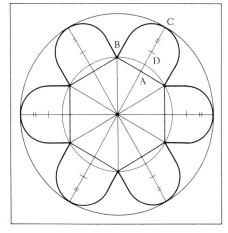

4

Using point D as the center, draw a half-circle whose radius is the AB measurement. Extend the ends of the half-circle to the corners of the hexagon. Repeat with remaining sides. Cut out the pattern.

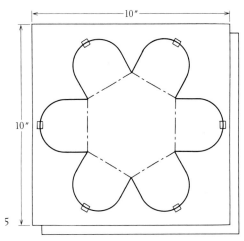

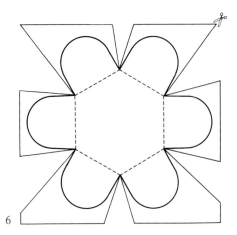

5 Lay the sheets of tracing paper together. Place the pattern on top in the center and fix in place with small pieces of removable tape. Firmly score the petal shapes and the sides of the hexagon.

6 Remove the pattern and cut notches between the petals.

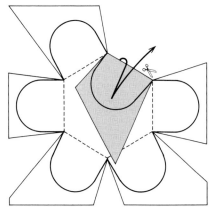

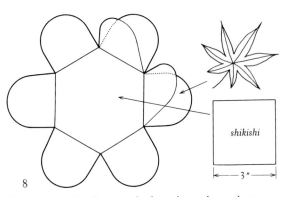

7 Carefully fold a petal inward along the side of the hexagon, crease firmly, and unfold. Repeat with remaining petals, making sure the paper does not slip. Cut out the petals.

8 Gently insert the flower or leaf you have chosen between the layers of tracing paper. Use the *shikishi* as is or cut it into a hexagon. Write your message on the *shikishi* and slide it in.

shikishi

—3"—

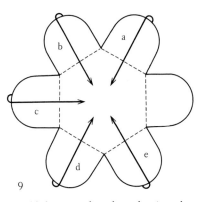

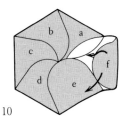

Tuck the edge of petal *f* under petal *a* as shown.

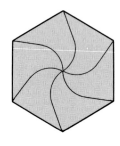

9 Fold down petals *a* through *e* in order.

Kraft Cards

In this series, kraft paper is used to achieve a casualness, making these cards ideal for change-of-address notices and other informal messages.
(Cards 12 through 16, pages 37–41.)

ou know why I'm sending
this card?
No reason at all
These colors
remind me of you.

Betty

Yoshi

Obi Cards

Hearts are for giving...
Be my Valentine?
Rene

A wide variety of cards, including squares, pentagons, and hexagons, can be made with long, beltlike strips of paper, a shape reminiscent of the
kimono's sash, or *obi*.

(Cards 17 through 26, pages 42–56.)

Casual Fanfares

These bright, cheerful, simple-to-make cards are just right for teens, young adults, or anyone young at heart.

(Cards 27 through 30, pages 57–60.)

12 Kraft Card

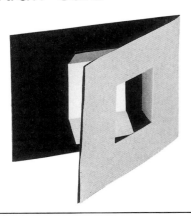

This card with its windowlike opening is ideal for change-of-address notices. Instead of the natural tones used here, yellow and navy blue, for example, could be combined for a bolder effect. Write the message around the window or take advantage of the unusual shape by writing your message on the flaps or under them so the message is visible only when you close the windows.

MATERIALS
1 piece 11½ × 4-inch tan kraft paper
1 piece 11½ × 4-inch red kraft paper

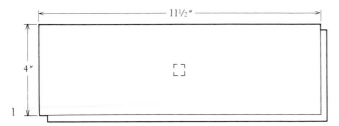

1   Position papers back to back, aligning the edges, and fix in place with a small piece of double-face tape.

2   With the tan side up, fold the paper in half.

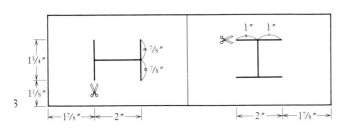

3   Unfold. Mark off the two H-shaped slits, then cut with a small utility knife to make windows.

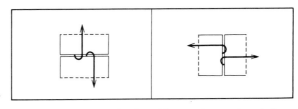

4   Score along the dotted lines and open the windows.

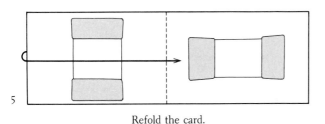

5   Refold the card.

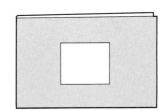

13 Kraft Card

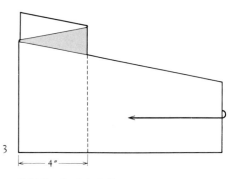

Unlike most of the cards in this book, which use two or more sheets of paper, this card is made of a single sheet. The sloping layers are pleasing and easy to make. Write your message in one fold or spread it across several.

MATERIAL

1 piece 7 × 20-inch parchment paper, semi-transparent-type

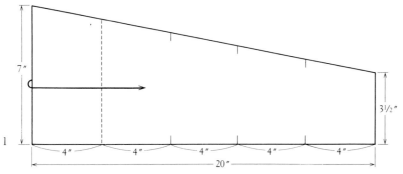

7″

3¹/₂″

1

4″   4″   4″   4″   4″

20″

Cut the paper into a trapezoid shape as shown. Mark off and score at 4-inch intervals. Fold the left edge in along the first line.

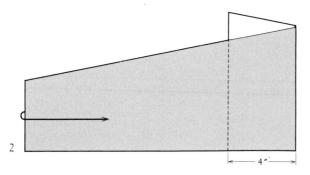

2

4″

Turn paper over. Fold back, aligning with edge underneath.

3

4″

Fold flap back to left.

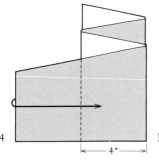

4

4″

Make last fold.

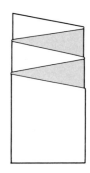

14 Kraft Card

The inspiration for this card came from the ziggurats, ancient temples shaped like terraced pyramids. The combination of the natural tan with navy blue or red gives the card a distinctive look. The message can be written inside or on the ziggurat face.

MATERIALS

1 piece 9 × 4¼-inch tan kraft paper
1 piece 9 × 4¼-inch red kraft paper

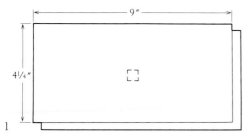

1 Position the papers back to back, aligning the edges, and fix in place with a small piece of double-face tape.

2 Place the red side up and trace the pattern (provided below) onto the paper as shown. (Do not score the center line yet.)

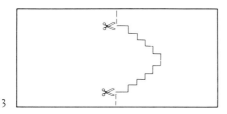

3 Cut the ziggurat pattern with a small utility knife, leaving the edges uncut. Score those uncut edges.

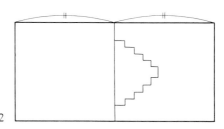

4 Fold the right side flap to the left along the scored center lines, leaving the ziggurat pattern flat.

5 Trim edges to match exactly.

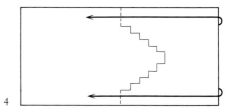

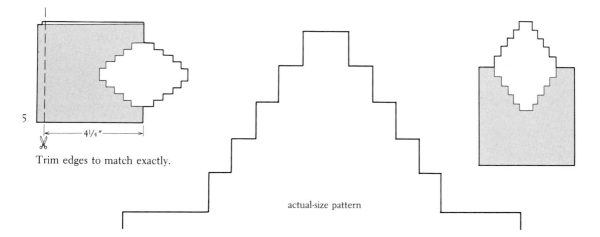

actual-size pattern

15 Kraft Card

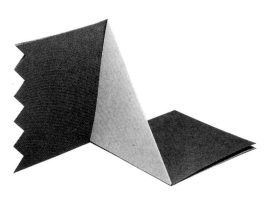

A *simple tan square tastefully edged with dark blue—that is all this card seems to be until it is opened; then it twists and almost unravels. Write your message with silver or white ink on the navy blue surface for dramatic flair.*

MATERIALS

1 piece 12½ × 4-inch tan kraft paper
1 piece 12½ × 4-inch navy blue kraft paper

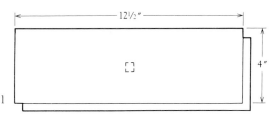

Position the papers back to back, aligning the edges, and fix in place with a small piece of double-face tape.

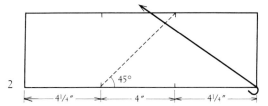

With blue side up, measure and score the diagonal line as shown. Fold right side up along line.

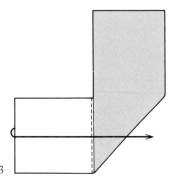

Place a ruler along the left edge of the flap folded in step 2 and firmly score the line to be folded. Fold the left flap to the right. Turn the paper over.

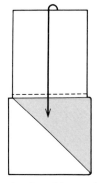

Score the dotted line and fold the upper flap down.

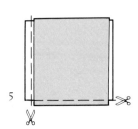

Trim the excess as shown.

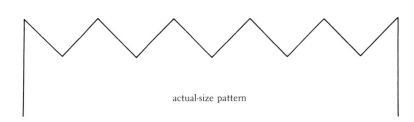

actual-size pattern

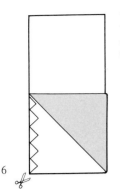

Unfold to position in step 4.
Trace the provided pattern
on the paper and cut as
shown.

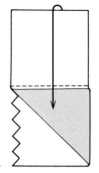

6

Fold the upper flap down again.

7

16 Kraft Card

*Two diagonal cuts suffice to create the lively, breezy
effect here. Use the triangular flap or the front of the
card for your name (see color plate) or the recipient's.*

MATERIALS
1 piece 12¾ × 4-inch tan kraft paper
1 piece 12¾ × 4-inch blue kraft paper

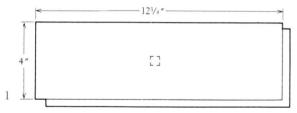

1

Position the papers back to back, aligning the edges,
and fix in place with a small piece of double-face tape.

2

With the blue side up,
fold the paper in half.

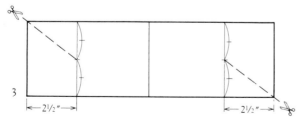

3

Unfold. Cut two diagonal
slits as shown.

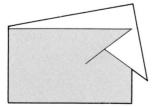

4

Refold the card, interlocking
the flaps as shown.

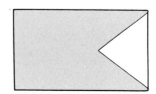

17 Obi Card

This chic hexagonal card presents the classic "cube illusion." The momigami (crinkled paper) softens the lines of the reversible design. Write your message wherever you like.

MATERIALS
1 piece 16 × 2⅛-inch brown *momigami* or any sturdy textured paper
1 piece 16 × 2⅛-inch silver paper

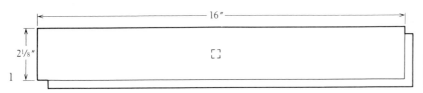

1

Position the papers back to back. Fix in place with a small piece of double-face tape at the center.

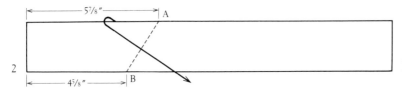

2

Mark points A and B. Fold along line AB. Turn paper over.

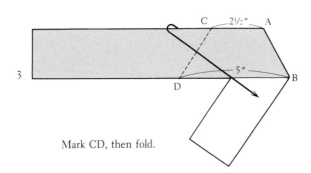

3

Mark CD, then fold.

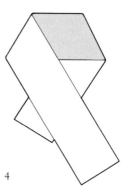

4

Press down folds firmly and make sure there is no gap at the center where the three layers meet.

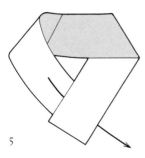

5

Slide the flap folded in step 3 under the other flap.

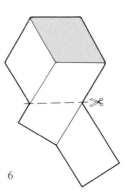

6

Cut away excess to make the "cube."

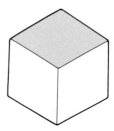

18 Obi Card

The colors here are modern and, along with the texture of the papers, give the card its personality. Unlike ordinary papers, Japanese paper gives a little, so adjust the shape of the pentagon as you go. Write your message on the inside face or on a separate card to be inserted in a fold of the finished card.

MATERIALS
1 piece 18½ × 3-inch gold paper
1 piece 18½ × 3-inch blue *momigami* or any sturdy textured paper

Position the papers back to back, and fix in place with a small piece of double-face tape at center.

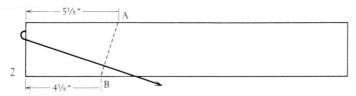

With the blue side face up, measure and mark points A and B, then score line AB and fold.

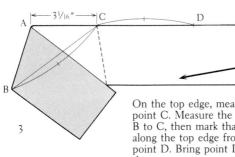

On the top edge, measure and mark point C. Measure the distance from B to C, then mark that same distance along the top edge from C to find point D. Bring point D to point B, then crease.

Card should look like this. Turn over.

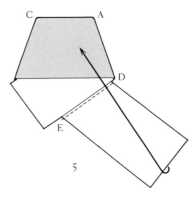

Score line DE and fold along the line as shown.

Insert the flap folded in step 5 as shown, creasing well.

6

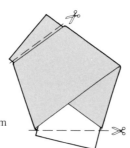

7
Trim the top and bottom to form pentagon.

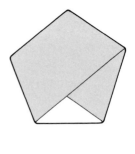

---

19 Obi Card

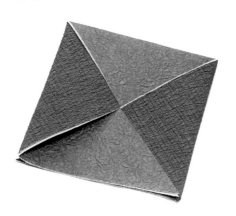

Chirimengami *and* momigami *are distinctive types of Japanese paper that have a natural warmth. This card is ideal for a short message to a spouse or a thank you card to grandparents or a close friend. Write your message on the inside, where it is not immediately visible.*

MATERIALS

1 piece 16½ × 3-inch brown *chirimengami* or any sturdy textured paper
1 piece 16½ × 3-inch blue *momigami* or any sturdy textured paper

---

16½″

3″

1

Position the papers back to back, and fix in place with a small piece of double-face tape.

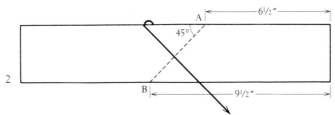

2

A ← 6½″ →
45°
B ← 9½″ →

Measure and mark line AB, then score and fold.

A

B

6″

C

Measure and mark point C, then score line BC and fold.

3

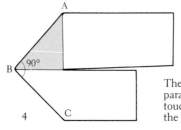

A

B 90°

C

4

The two folded flaps should be parallel, and the edges should touch but not overlap. Turn the paper over.

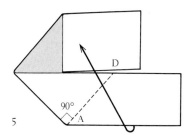

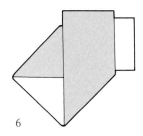

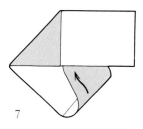

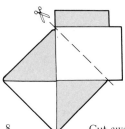

5 Measure and mark point D, then score line AD and fold lower flap up.

6 Card should look like this.

7 Slide the flap folded in step 5 under other flap.

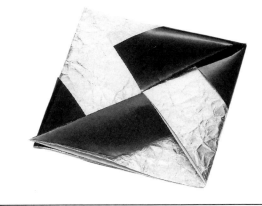

8 Cut away excess to make square.

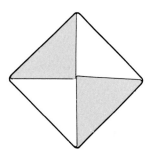

20 Obi Card

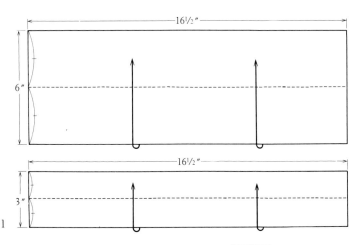

This variation on Card 19 was inspired by the striking costumes and colors of the kabuki theater. The wonderfully bold contrast between the silver Japanese paper and ordinary black paper adds impact and interest.

MATERIALS
1 piece 16½ × 6-inch silver *momigami* or any sturdy textured paper
1 piece 16½ × 3-inch black paper

16½"

6"

16½"

3"

1 Fold both papers in half along the length.

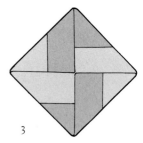

black

silver

2

Position black paper over silver paper. Fix in place with a small piece of double-face tape at the center.

3

To complete the card, follow the instructions for Card 19, beginning with step 2.

21 Obi Card

This card uses basic chiyogami *patterned papers. You can easily vary the overall mood of the card by changing the hue. To accentuate the pattern, choose papers of similar hue. Write your message on the tissue before inserting it between the strips of* chiyogami.

MATERIALS
1 piece 14 × 2⅝-inch blue *chiyogami*
1 piece 14 × 2⅝-inch black *chiyogami*
1 piece 14 × 2⅝-inch tissue

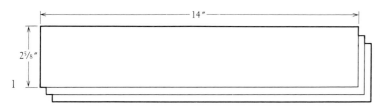

14″

2⅝″

1

Position *chiyogami* papers back to back, and slide tissue between them.

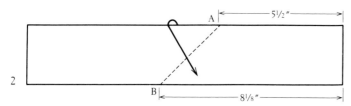

A

5½″

B

8⅛″

2

Measure and mark points A and B, then score line AB and fold.

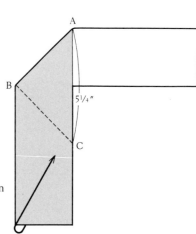

A

B

5¼″

C

3

Measure and mark point C, then score line BC and fold.

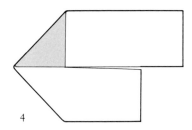

4

The two folded flaps should be parallel and
the edges should touch but not overlap.
Turn the paper over.

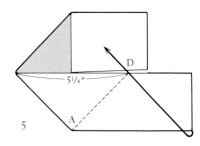

5

Measure and mark point D. Score line AD
and fold lower flap up along the line.

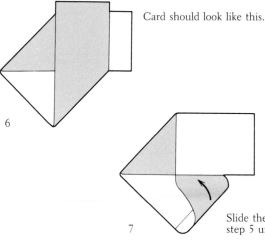

6

Card should look like this.

7

Slide the flap folded in
step 5 under the other.

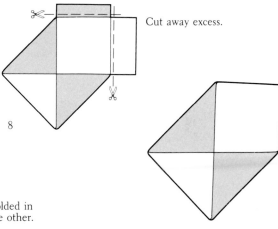

8

Cut away excess.

22 Obi Card

The combination of ocher and blue or red is typical of
Edo (shogun-era Tokyo) city taste. The overall impression is casual, so you can use it for any informal
purpose. Try substituting chiyogami for one of the
papers. Write your message on the inside.

MATERIALS

1 piece 14 × 2⅛-inch ocher *momigami* or any
  sturdy textured paper
1 piece 14 × 2⅛-inch red *momigami* or any sturdy
  textured paper

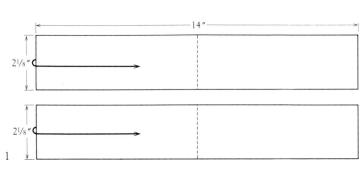

1

With colored sides down, fold both
sheets in half.

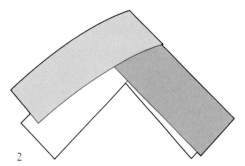

2

Insert one half of one strip inside the other to form an L. Be sure the two sheets form a right angle at the corner.

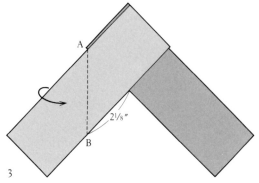

3

Mark point B, then fold left side in along line AB.

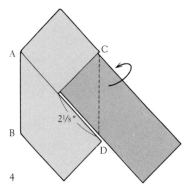

4

Mark point D and fold along line CD parallel to line AB.

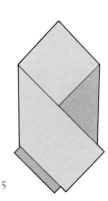

5

Card should look like this.

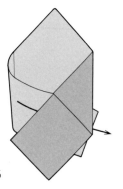

6

Slide top flap under the other flap.

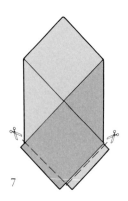

7

Cut away excess as shown.

23 Obi Card

The two joined pentagons that form this card depict the knot of the obi, a kimono sash. The traditional hemp-leaf-patterned chiyogami and gold Japanese paper recall love letters from older times, but the appeal is entirely modern. To ensure clean, neat pentagons, adjust the knots carefully.

MATERIALS
1 strip 20 × 1½-inch gold paper
1 strip 20 × 1½-inch red *chiyogami*
1 piece 4¾ × 4¾-inch medium-weight white tracing paper

1 Position the gold and the patterned papers back to back. Fix in place with a small piece of double-face tape at the center.

2 With gold side face up, measure and mark points A and B. Fold along line AB.

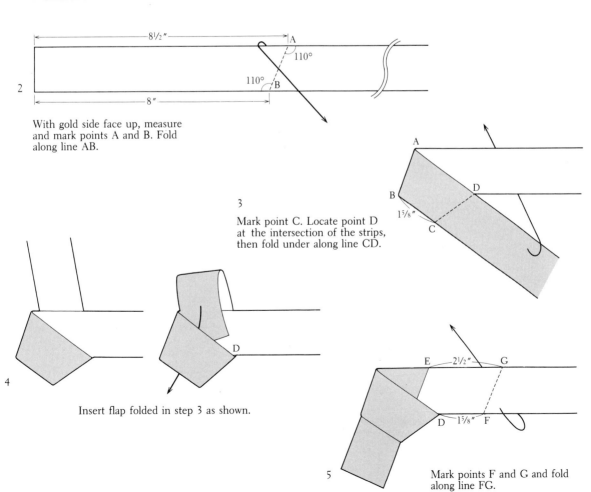

3 Mark point C. Locate point D at the intersection of the strips, then fold under along line CD.

4 Insert flap folded in step 3 as shown.

5 Mark points F and G and fold along line FG.

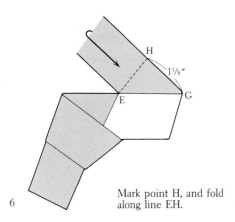

6   Mark point H, and fold along line EH.

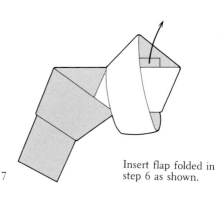

7   Insert flap folded in step 6 as shown.

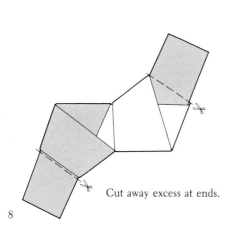

8   Cut away excess at ends.

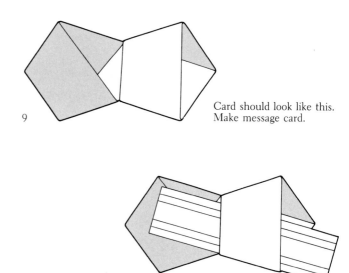

9   Card should look like this. Make message card.

MESSAGE CARD   On the tracing paper, mark off the intervals shown and make a series of fan folds starting from the widest fold. Write your message and insert in the folds of the card.

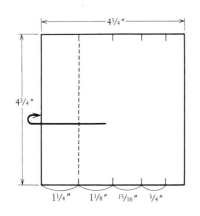

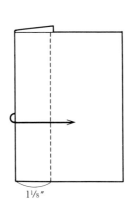

For message cards for Cards 24 and 26, follow the same steps, using the measurements given in Card 24.

24 Obi Card

An obi *knotted into three pentagons makes a fanciful birthday or gift card, or an eye-catching bookmark. Make the message card of tracing paper.*

MATERIALS

1 strip 20 × 1⅛-inch red *momigami* or any sturdy textured paper

1 strip 20 × 1⅛-inch silver *momigami* or any sturdy textured paper

1 piece 4¾ × 3⅞-inch medium-weight white tracing paper

1   Place the red paper and silver paper back to back, and fix in place with a small piece of double-face tape at center.

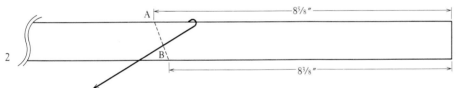

2   With silver side face up, mark points A and B, then fold along line AB.

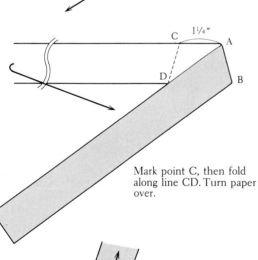

3   Mark point C, then fold along line CD. Turn paper over.

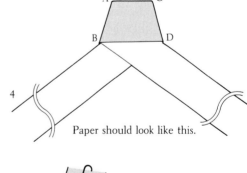

4   Paper should look like this.

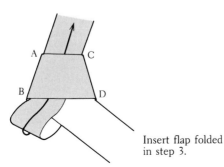

5   Insert flap folded in step 3.

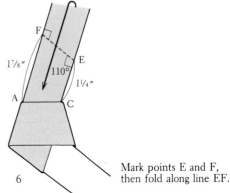

6   Mark points E and F, then fold along line EF.

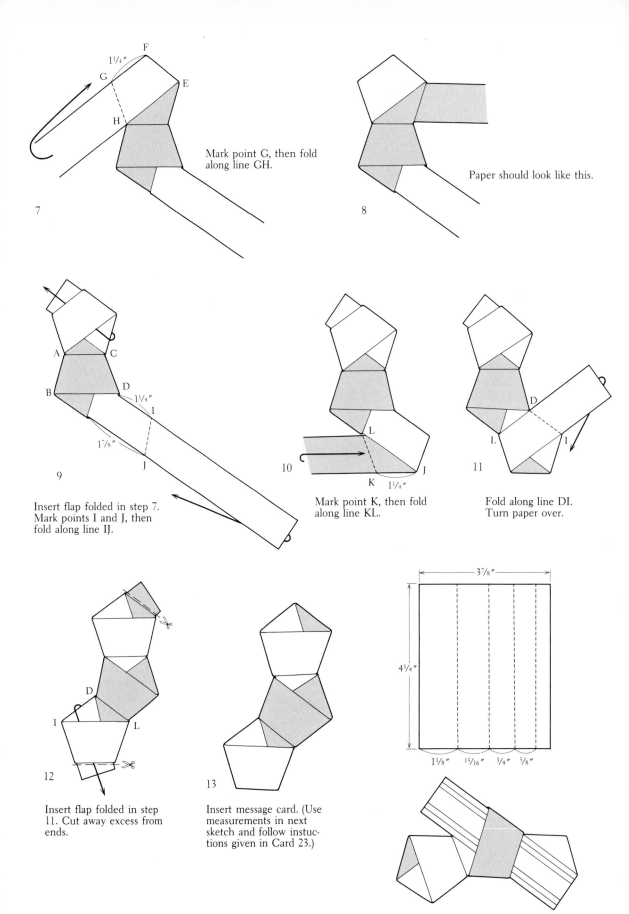

7

Mark point G, then fold along line GH.

8

Paper should look like this.

9

Insert flap folded in step 7. Mark points I and J, then fold along line IJ.

10

Mark point K, then fold along line KL.

11

Fold along line DI. Turn paper over.

12

Insert flap folded in step 11. Cut away excess from ends.

13

Insert message card. (Use measurements in next sketch and follow instuctions given in Card 23.)

25 Obi Card

Inspiration for this card came from Japanese paper bridal dolls. You'll find many creative uses for this card. It is, for example, soon inserted in a book or other borrowed item you are returning, with a short note of thanks. Write your message on the tail.

MATERIALS

1 strip 18 × 1⅛-inch purple *chiyogami*
1 strip 18 × 1⅛-inch green *chiyogami*

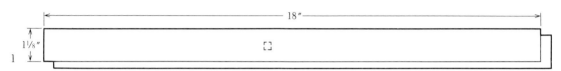

1 Position the papers back to back. Align the edges and fix paper in place with a small piece of double-face tape about 8 inches from the left edge.

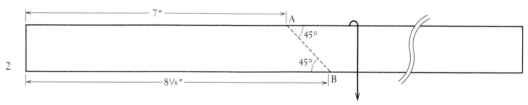

2 With purple side face up, mark points A and B, then fold right flap down along line AB. Rotate the paper so A is at left.

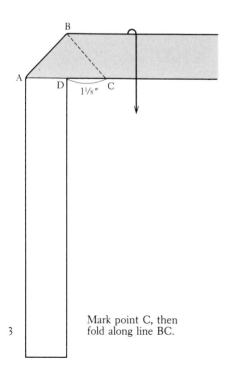

3 Mark point C, then fold along line BC.

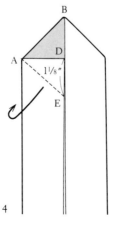

4 Mark point E, then fold back along AE.

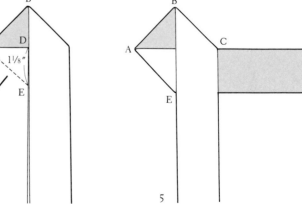

5 Paper should look like this.

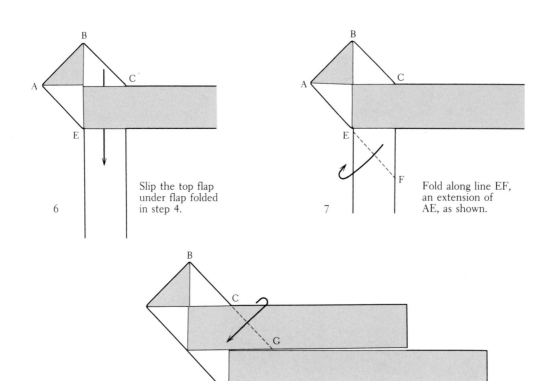

6   Slip the top flap
under flap folded
in step 4.

7   Fold along line EF,
an extension of
AE, as shown.

8   Fold along line CG, an extension of BC,
as shown.

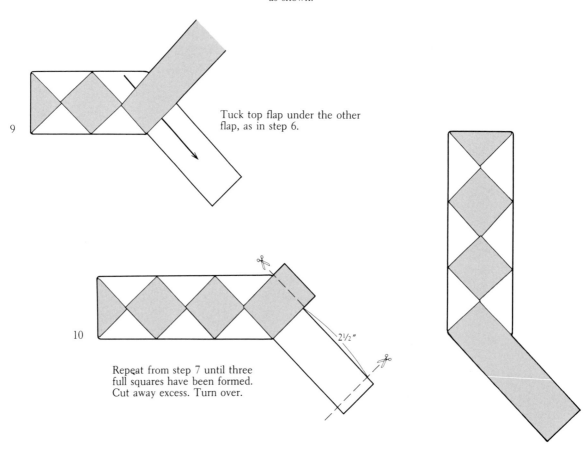

9   Tuck top flap under the other
flap, as in step 6.

10   Repeat from step 7 until three
full squares have been formed.
Cut away excess. Turn over.

2½″

26 Obi Card

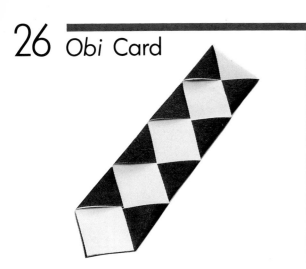

The textural contrast here between Japanese paper and ordinary paper of the same color creates a smart, modern appeal. Keep the series of simple folds tight to ensure a neat and clean finish. Insert a message card made of tracing paper.

MATERIALS
1 strip 21 × 1⅛-inch plain red paper
1 strip 21 × 1⅛-inch red *momigami* or any sturdy textured paper
1 piece 4¾ × 3⅞-inch medium-weight white tracing paper

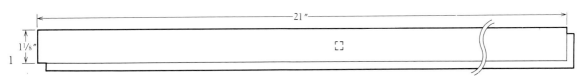

1 Position the red papers back to back. Fix in place with a small piece of double-face tape about 10 inches from the left end.

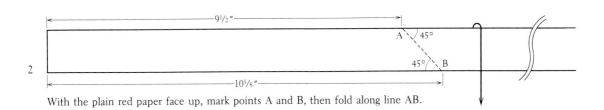

2 With the plain red paper face up, mark points A and B, then fold along line AB.

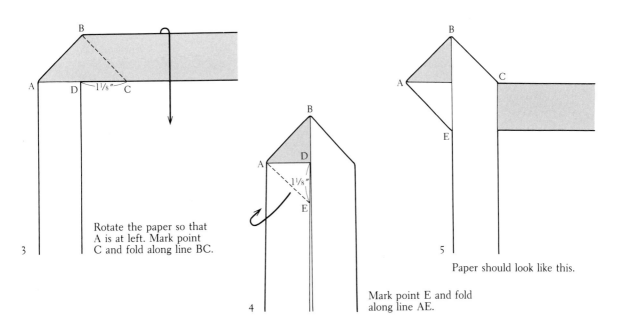

3 Rotate the paper so that A is at left. Mark point C and fold along line BC.

4 Mark point E and fold along line AE.

5 Paper should look like this.

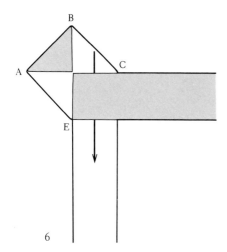

6

Slip the top flap under the other.

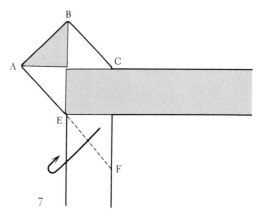

7

Fold line EF, which is an extension of line AE.

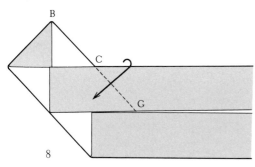

8

Fold line CG, an extension of line BC.

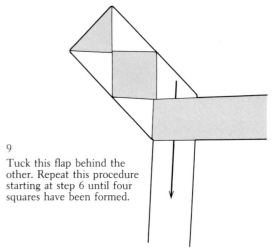

9

Tuck this flap behind the other. Repeat this procedure starting at step 6 until four squares have been formed.

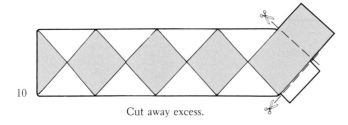

10

Cut away excess.

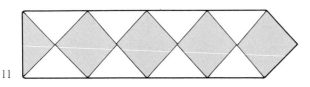

11

Insert message card. (Instructions for message card are with Card 23.)

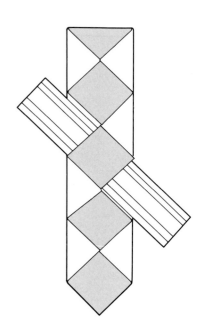

27 Casual Fanfare

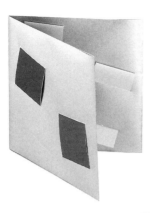

Any color looks good against the silver background of this card, so follow your own inclination when making the four message cards. Position the slits as you like, as long as the inserted message cards form squares on the front and back of the card.

MATERIALS

1 piece 16 × 4-inch silver paper
1 piece 4¾ × 1⅛-inch pink paper
1 piece 4¾ × 1⅛-inch yellow paper
1 piece 4¾ × 1⅛-inch purple paper
1 piece 4¾ × 1⅛-inch white paper

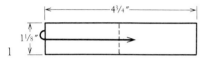

Make four small message cards by folding the small papers in half.

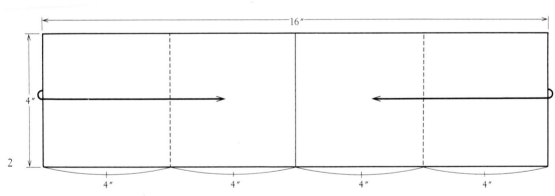

Place silver side of large paper face down, then fold right and left edges to meet at the center as shown.

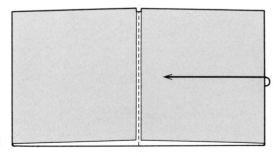

Fold in half at center.

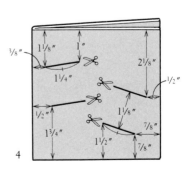

Mark and cut slits as shown. Cut through all four layers of paper. Unfold to position in step 3.

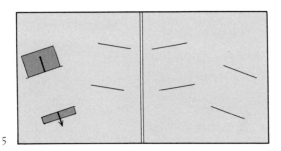

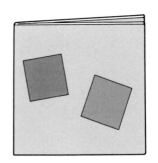

5 Card should look like this. Insert the message cards in the slits. Refold.

28 Casual Fanfare

The see-through quality of the tracing paper, the woven effect, and the softness of the colors under their translucent cover give this card an air of light sophistication. Since one message card faces in and the other out, you can heighten interest by starting your message on the outside and completing it on the inside.

MATERIALS
1 piece 8 × 5-inch heavyweight white tracing paper
1 piece 4¾ × 1⅛-inch pink paper
1 piece 4¾ × 1⅛-inch orange paper

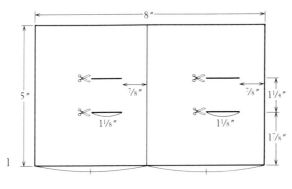

1 Measure, mark, and cut four slits as shown.

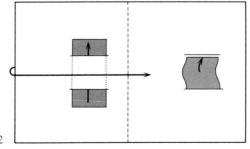

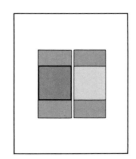

2 Make message cards by folding pink and orange papers in half (see Card 27), and insert them in the slits. Fold the card in half.

29 Casual Fanfare

The bright colors muted by the tracing paper lend a dreamy touch to this light, airy card. Unique and original effects are easy to create by simply varying the position and hue of the message cards.

MATERIALS

1 piece 8 × 5-inch heavyweight white tracing paper
1 piece 4¾ × 1⅛-inch green paper
1 piece 4¾ × 1⅛-inch yellow paper

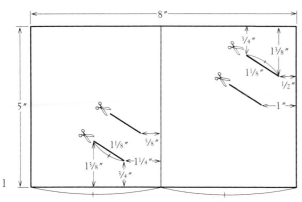

Measure, mark, and cut four slits as shown.

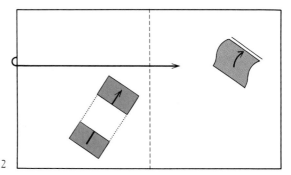

Make message cards by folding the green and yellow papers in half (see Card 27). Insert in the slits, then fold the card in half.

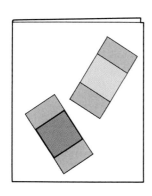

30 Casual Fanfare

For this card choose lively, contrasting colors such as yellow, pink, green, and blue, or personalize your creation by using your recipient's favorite colors.

MATERIALS
1 piece 9½ × 2⅜-inch pink paper
1 piece 9½ × 2⅜-inch silver paper
1 piece 4¾ × 1⅛-inch yellow paper

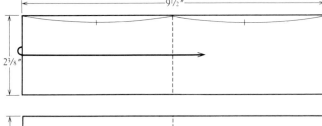

Place pink paper face down and fold in half. Repeat with silver paper.

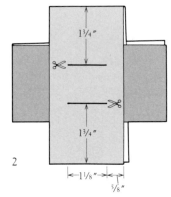

2

Cross papers, fixing in place with removable tape. Cut two slits through the four layers, following the measurements exactly. Remove the tape.

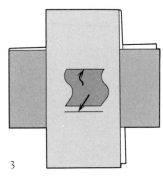

3

Make the message card by folding the small yellow paper in half (see Card 27). Insert it in the slits as shown to hold the layers together.

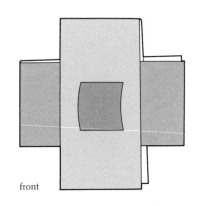

front

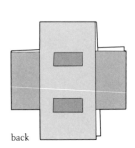

back

Baby Cards

These fresh, delicate cards employ pale and gentle colors to evoke the innocence of a newborn baby and the soft fullness of an infant's blanket.

(Cards 31 through 34, pages 65–68.)

Christmas Cards

The red of Santa's suit, the green of the Christmas tree, and the gold of the star—all colors that say "Merry Christmas" and are used in all these cards to help convey your season's greetings.

(Cards 35 through 44, pages 69–82.)

Wedding Cards

Your joy will double...

Congratulations and best wishes!

Chris and John

Congratulations on taking the big step!

Jack Straw

These elegant cards in subtle shades of champagne, pale blue, and serene gold are perfect for expressing congratulations to newlyweds.

(Cards 45 through 48, pages 83–87.)

31 Baby Card

The next two cards represent a receiving blanket, a fitting shape for a birth announcement or to accompany a baby gift. The gold paper conveys the importance of the occasion, while the tracing paper softens the tone. Unify the whole by writing your message in gold ink so that it peeks out from the folds.

MATERIALS

1 piece 8 × 8-inch medium-weight pink tracing paper
1 piece 7¾ × 7¾-inch gold paper
1 piece 7½ × 7½-inch medium-weight white tracing paper
pink, gold, and gray threads

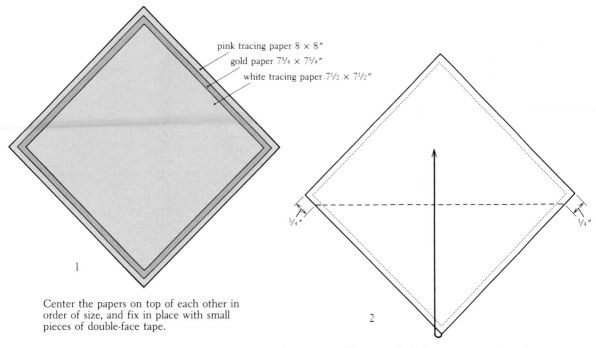

pink tracing paper 8 × 8″
gold paper 7¾ × 7¾″
white tracing paper 7½ × 7½″

¾″   ¾″

1

Center the papers on top of each other in order of size, and fix in place with small pieces of double-face tape.

2

Turn over. Fold bottom tip up along a line ¾ of an inch below the widest point.

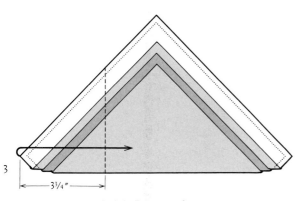

3   3¾″

Fold left flap toward center.

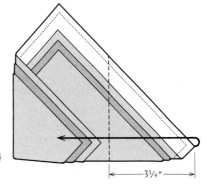

4   3¾″

Fold right flap toward center.

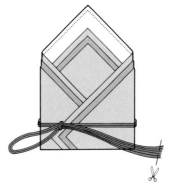

Wrap the threads together around the card and tie in a bow. Trim ends.

5

32 Baby Card

Here is a variation on the preceding card. The taped papers are simply turned over a second time before the final folds are made.

MATERIALS

1 piece 8 × 8-inch medium-weight green tracing paper

1 piece 7¾ × 7¾-inch gold paper

1 piece 7½ × 7½-inch medium-weight white tracing paper

blue, gold, and white threads

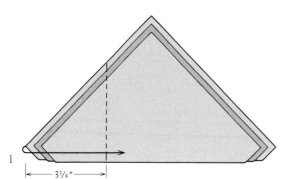

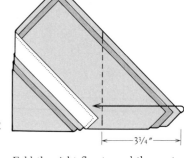

1

├─── 3¾ " ───┤

Follow steps 1 and 2 of previous card. Turn the paper over again. Fold the left flap toward the center as shown.

2

├─── 3¾ " ───┤

Fold the right flap toward the center.

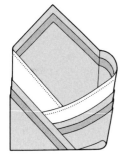

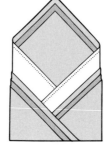

3

Insert right flap between the layers of the left flap.

4

Card should look like this.

5

Wrap the threads together around the card and tie a bow. Trim ends.

33 Baby Card

The widening form of the fan denotes growing prosperity to the Japanese, who often use it for celebratory occasions. The pale yellow paper creates an impression of freshness, to which your message itself becomes a design accent.

MATERIALS
1 piece 8 × 3⅞-inch pale pink medium-weight
    tracing paper
gold thread

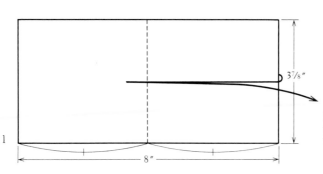

1

First write a message horizontally across the width of the top third of the paper, then fold in half. Unfold.

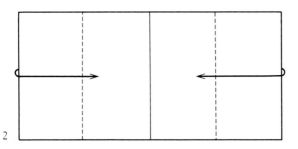

2

Fold right and left edges in to center line.

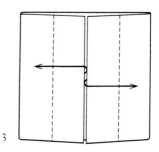

3

Fold center edges back to the outer edges.

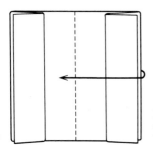

4

Fold in half, bringing the doubled outside edges together.

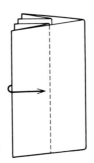

5

Fold top flap back.

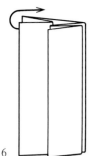

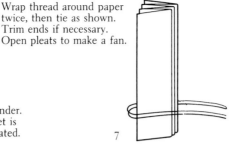

Wrap thread around paper twice, then tie as shown. Trim ends if necessary. Open pleats to make a fan.

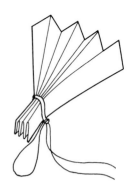

6

Fold left flap under. The entire sheet is now evenly pleated.

7

34 Baby Card

Overlapping layers of tracing paper blend together in this card to produce subtle color effects. Give it a delicate finish by tying it with coordinating threads rather than a wide ribbon. Write your message on the center of the inside surface.

MATERIALS

1 piece 6 × 4¼-inch medium-weight white tracing paper
1 piece 6 × 4¼-inch medium-weight yellow tracing paper
1 piece 6 × 4¼-inch medium-weight green tracing paper
gold, blue, and white threads

green
yellow
white

1

Position papers on top of each other as shown.

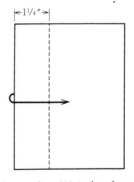

2

Score a line 1¼ inches from the left edge. Fold.

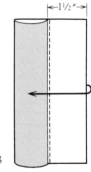

3

Score a line 1½ inches from the right edge. Fold.

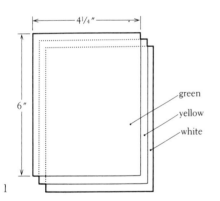

green
yellow
white

4

Slide the papers out at the top as shown. Rotate so seam is at back.

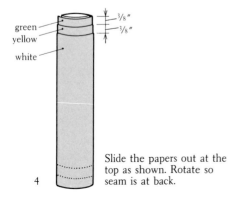

5

Combine the threads. Wrap around paper and tie.

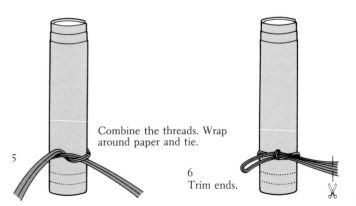

6
Trim ends.

35 Christmas Card

Although this card uses simple napkin folds, the effect is splendid. Taking a cue from Japanese New Year decorations, fine strands of gold and red are threaded through the card and tied. A message in gold forms an effective complement to the red surface (see color plate). For best results, press the first fold firmly but the others gently.

MATERIALS
1 piece 9 × 9-inch gold paper
1 piece 9 × 9-inch red paper
red and gold strands

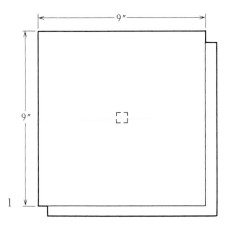

1 Position sheets of paper back to back. Fix in place with a small piece of double-face tape at the center.

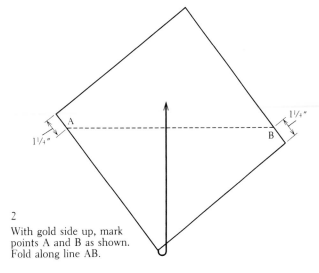

2 With gold side up, mark points A and B as shown. Fold along line AB.

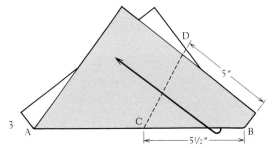

3 Mark points C and D, then fold along line CD.

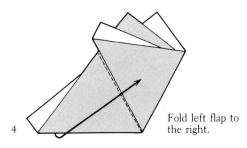

4 Fold left flap to the right.

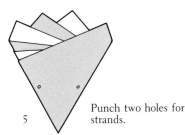

5 Punch two holes for strands.

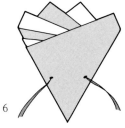

6 Thread strands through holes, then tie in a bow. Trim ends if necessary.

36 Christmas Card

Formed with accordion folds at its center, this card nonetheless has a stylish flair. Because of its simplicity, the creases must be sharp and crisp. The more care you put into it, the more beautiful the result will be. Write your message on the inside of the side flap.

MATERIALS
2 pieces 10 × 4-inch red paper
gold strands

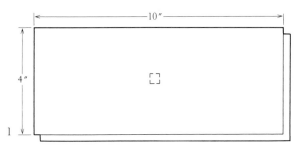

Position sheets of paper back to back and fix in place with a small piece of double-face tape at the center.

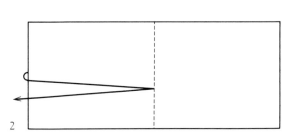

Fold in half at center. Unfold.

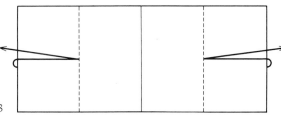

Fold each end into the center. Unfold.

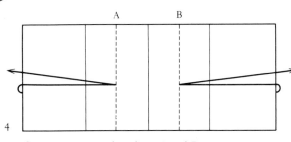

Crease center panels at lines A and B.

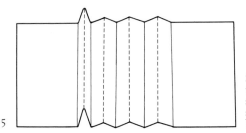

Spreading the paper out and starting from the left crease, bring the first crease to the second, the second to the third, and so on, so that you have an accordion spine on a book-type card.

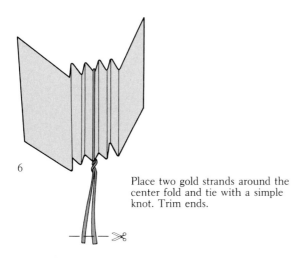

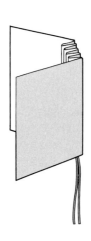

6

Place two gold strands around the center fold and tie with a simple knot. Trim ends.

37 Christmas Card

This card resembles a kite, with the gold strand tied around the center forming its "tail." Making the tapered fan-folds requires great care. Score the lines precisely so the kite effect will not be distorted. Write your message on the inside of the side flap.

MATERIALS
2 pieces 10 × 3½-inch red paper
gold strands

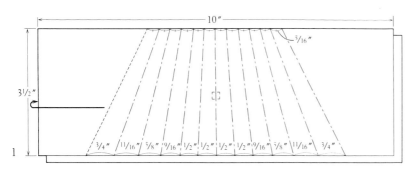

10"

5/16"

3½"

1

¾" 11/16" 5/8" 9/16" 1/2" 1/2" 1/2" 1/2" 9/16" 5/8" 11/16" ¾"

Position papers back to back and fix in place with a small piece of double-face tape at the center. Score lines starting from the center as shown. Begin by folding the far left line.

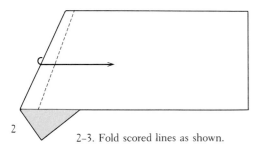

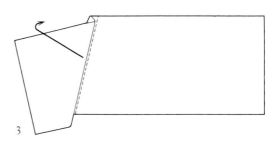

2

3

2–3. Fold scored lines as shown.

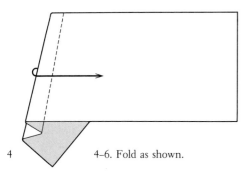

4

4–6. Fold as shown.

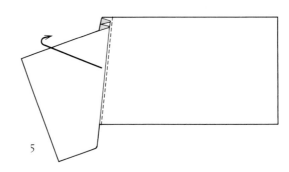

5

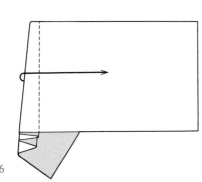

6

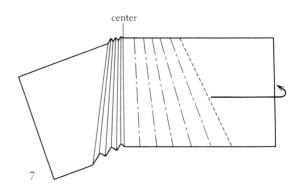

center

7

When you reach the center, start folding from the right in the same way.

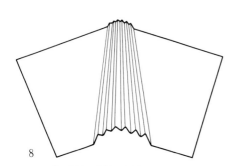

8

Card should look like this. This face will be the outside of the card. Turn paper over.

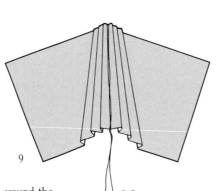

9

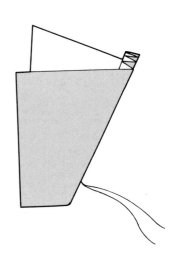

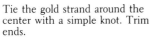

Tie the gold strand around the center with a simple knot. Trim ends.

38 Christmas Card

The sophisticated balance of staggered shelves in the display alcoves of traditional Japanese homes provides the inspiration for this contemporary card. Two off-center overlapping panels open to reveal a pentagonal *obi* knot. To ensure a perfect fit, make the pentagon before cutting the slits into which it will slide. Write your message wherever you like.

MATERIALS

1 piece 13 × 3¼-inch silver paper
1 piece 13 × 3¼-inch green paper
2 strips 10 × ⅞-inch red paper

Place silver paper and green paper face down and fold in half.

13″

3¼″

silver

3¼″

green

1

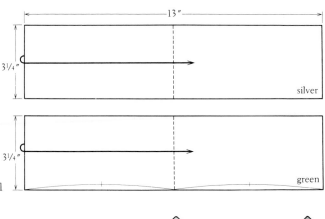

2

Fold each in half again.

silver   ⅞″   90°   green

Open papers halfway, then insert green paper at right angles between layers of silver paper, ⅞ inch off center.

3

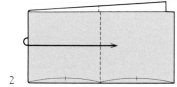

10″

⅞″   4⅛″   A   red

3⅞″   B

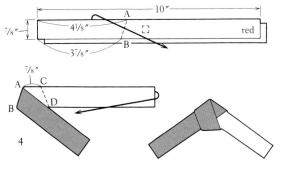

⅞″

A   C

B   D

4

Make a pentagonal *obi* knot out of red paper, following steps 2 through 6 for Card 23 but using the measurements given here.

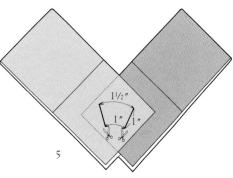

1½″

1″   1″

5

Mark the ends of the cutting lines by puncturing with a needle. With a small utility knife, cut through all four layers using a ruler as a guide to make clean, straight cuts.

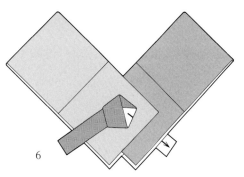

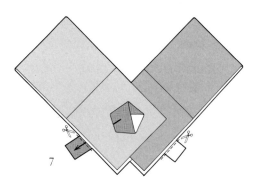

6

Insert the ends of the belt through the slits, widening if necessary.

7

Cut away the excess.

8

Fold over the green paper, then the silver paper.

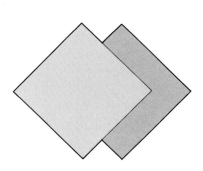

39 Christmas Card

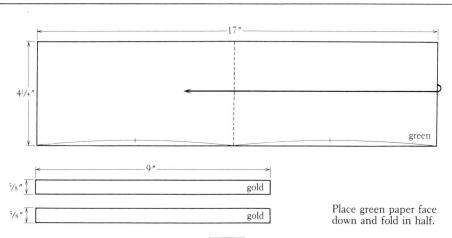

The red ribbon running through the center of this card lends a cheerful seasonal accent. The cutting lines do not have to be absolutely straight. Write one word of your message in each white space inside.

MATERIALS

1 piece 17 × 4¼-inch green paper
2 strips 9 × ⅝-inch gold paper
32-inch length of ½-inch red ribbon

17"

4¼"

green

9"

⅝" gold

1 ⅝" gold

Place green paper face down and fold in half.

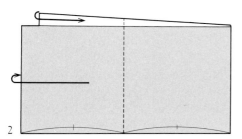

2

Fold each half in half.

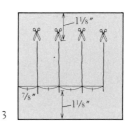

3

Use a needle to mark the ends of the cutting lines as shown, then use a utility knife to cut the slits free-hand through all layers of the paper.

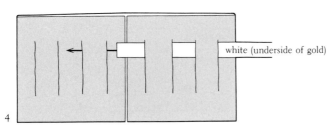

4

Open the paper halfway. Weave one strip of gold paper, face down, through the slits.

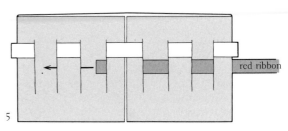

5

Slide the red ribbon through the slits to achieve a woven effect.

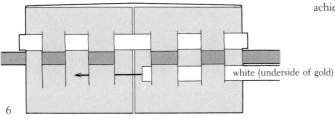

6

Weave the second strip of gold paper, face down, through the slits as in step 4.

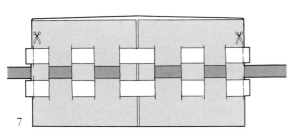

7

Cut away excess from ends of gold papers.

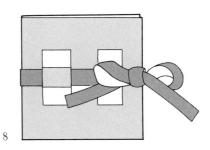

8

Fold card in half at center and tie the ribbon into a bow. Trim ends.

40 Christmas Card

The bold layers of green, red, and silver result in a card that is decidedly adult in character. It is designed so that when it is opened, the silver belt pops up inside, but it won't work unless the belt fits exactly, so be sure to test it.

MATERIALS
1 piece 16 × 2¾-inch green paper
1 strip 19 × ⅞-inch silver paper
1 strip 7 × 1⅞-inch red paper

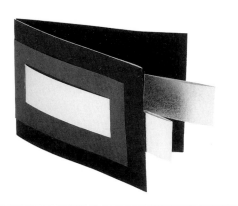

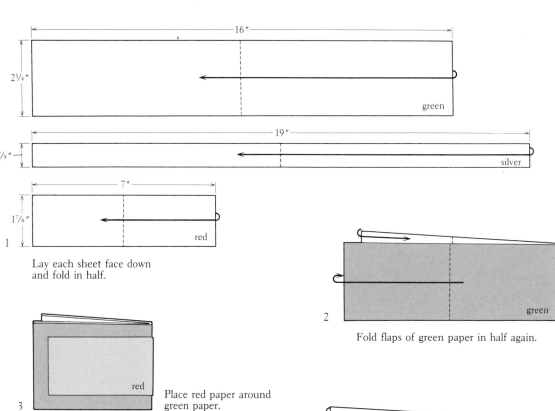

1 Lay each sheet face down and fold in half.

2 Fold flaps of green paper in half again.

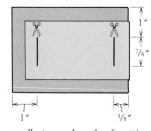

3 Place red paper around green paper.

4 Use a needle to mark ends of cutting lines by puncturing all layers. Cut from point to point through all layers, using a ruler to guide your utility knife.

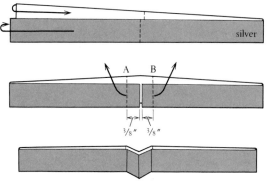

5 Fold both ends of the silver paper in half again. Mark lines A and B, then fold as shown. Turn over.

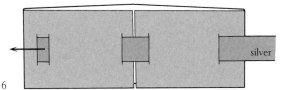

Open green paper as shown and
slide silver paper through the slits.

6

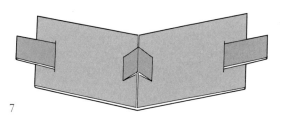

7

Align the center of the silver paper with
the center fold of the card. Refold.

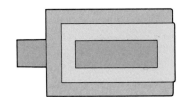

41 Christmas Card

*Decorations on the message card will appear to stand
in a silver landscape. Use the ample space on both sides
of the card to write your message, or use the inside of
the message card.*

MATERIALS
1 piece $17\frac{1}{2} \times 4\frac{3}{8}$-inch red paper
1 piece $17\frac{1}{2} \times 4\frac{3}{8}$-inch pearl white paper
1 strip $6 \times 1\frac{1}{2}$-inch green paper

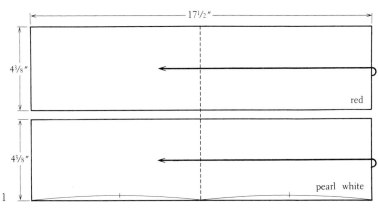

$17\frac{1}{2}$"

$4\frac{3}{8}$"

red

6"

$1\frac{1}{2}$"

green

$4\frac{3}{8}$"

pearl white

1

Place each paper face down and
fold in half.

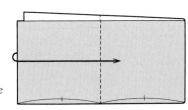

2
Fold red paper and white
paper in half again.

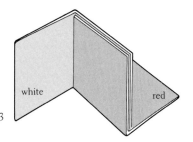

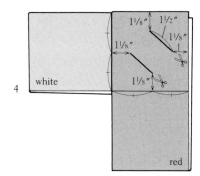

Use a needle to mark ends of the cutting lines, then cut through both sheets with a small utility knife, using a ruler as a guide for clean, straight cuts.

1 1/8" 1 1/2" 1 1/8" 1 1/8" 1 1/8"

4 white

red

3 Place white paper and red paper together as shown.

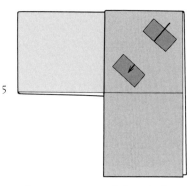

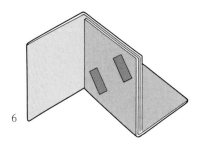

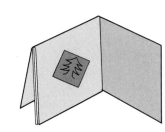

5 Insert message card through the slits, folded edge first.

6 Return card to position in step 3. Fold in flaps.

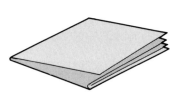

42 Christmas Card

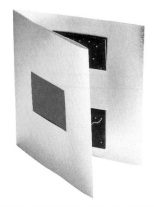

Add an extra touch to this urbane card by drawing illustrations in gold on the message cards. The silver background represents a field of snow in which the colored cards float in vivid contrast. Because the design is so simple, take special care with the execution.

MATERIALS
1 piece 17 1/2 × 4 3/8-inch silver paper
1 strip 7 × 1 7/8-inch red paper
1 strip 7 × 1 7/8-inch green paper

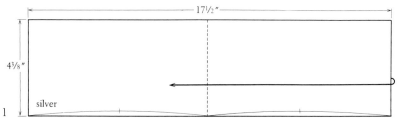

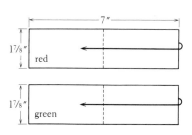

17 1/2"

4 3/8"

1 silver

7"

1 7/8" red

1 7/8" green

Lay silver paper face down and fold in half. Fold red paper and green paper in half in the same way.

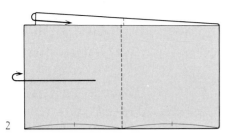

2

Fold both ends of the silver paper in half again.

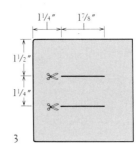

1¼" 1⅞"

1½"

1¼"

3

Mark ends of cutting lines by puncturing all layers with a needle. Cut from point to point through all layers using a ruler to guide your utility knife for clean, straight cuts. Be careful that the layers of paper do not slip.

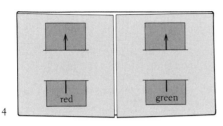

red

green

4

Open silver paper halfway. Insert green paper into right side slits, folded edge first. Insert red paper in the same way on the left side. Fold in half.

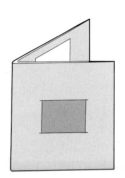

43 Christmas Card

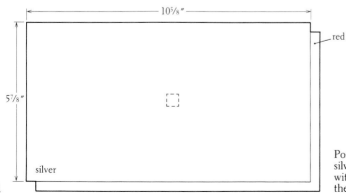

When this tiny package-of-a-card is opened up, an accordion-like message pops out. Multiply the effect by putting one word on each fold of the message card. The red of the message card reflects beautifully on the silver interior.

MATERIALS
1 piece 10⅝ × 5⅞-inch red paper
1 piece 10⅝ × 5⅞-inch silver paper
1 piece 21 × 4-inch red paper

10⅝"

red

5⅞"

silver

1

Position matching sheets of red paper and silver paper back to back, and fix in place with a small piece of double-face tape at the center.

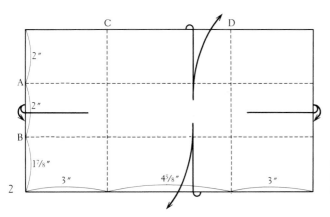

2

With silver side up, fold and unfold along lines A, B, C, and D in sequence.

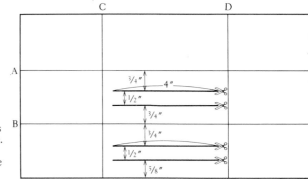

3

Lay paper flat. Mark ends of cut lines as shown by puncturing with a needle. With a small utility knife, cut from point to point using a ruler as a guide for clean, straight cuts.

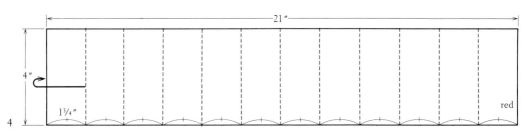

4

Place remaining red paper face up, and fan-fold at 1¾-inch intervals, starting from left edge. Write your message on the fan folds.

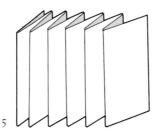

5

Paper should look like this.

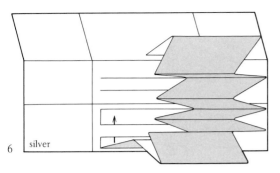 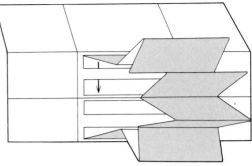

6 silver

Insert ends of the fan-folded paper into
the slits made in step 3.

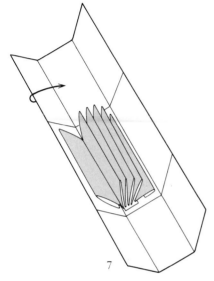

7

Fold left side (with slits) in.

8

Fold top (without slits) down.

9

Fold left end under.

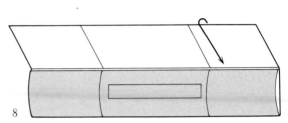

10

Fold right end under. Turn paper over.

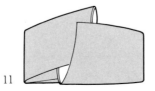 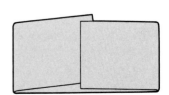

11

Insert left flap into right flap.

44 Christmas Card

Open this card and an elaborate red and silver design unfolds, reminiscent of the white Japanese crane with its accents of black and red. Send your message on the "wings" of this "crane."

MATERIALS
1 piece 8¾ × 4⅜-inch silver paper
1 piece 8¾ × 4⅜-inch red paper

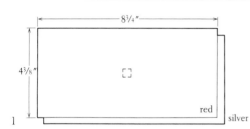

1 Position sheets back to back and fix in place with a small piece of double-face tape at the center.

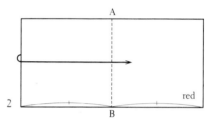

2 With red side up, fold in half along line AB to make a square.

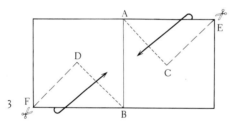

3 Open up again. Mark lines CE and DF from centers to corners and cut, using a small utility knife. Fold along lines AC and BD.

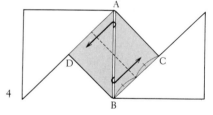

4 Fold back tips of triangular flaps.

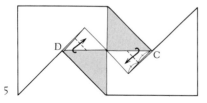

5 Again fold back tips of triangular flaps.

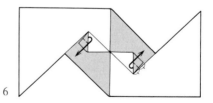

6 Again fold back half of flaps.

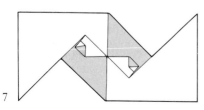

7 Card should look like this.

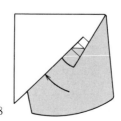

8 Fold the card in half, tucking the right flap behind the left to form a square.

45 Wedding Card

This card's restrained colors and elegant gold cord blend to create a genteel image. Tie cord with a simple knot for a crisp, unfussy look. If the folded lines are not parallel, the effect of purity will be spoiled, so make the folds with care. Use gold ink to write your message line by line on the inside panels.

MATERIALS
1 piece 17½ × 6¼-inch light blue paper
1 piece 17½ × 6¼-inch copper paper
gold cord

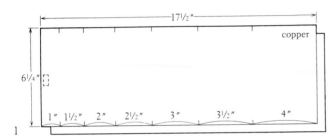

Position sheets of paper back to back and fix in place with a small piece of double-face tape at the left edge.

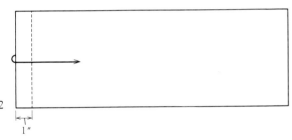

With copper side up, fold along the line 1 inch from the left edge. To achieve a sharp crease, lay a ruler along the fold line and gently but firmly fold over the entire flap at once. Be sure to make only one crease as you fold.

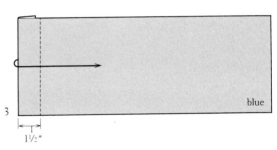

Turn paper over top to bottom, keeping folded part at the left. Fold along a line 1½ inches from left edge, keeping the fold lines parallel.

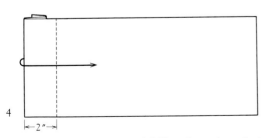

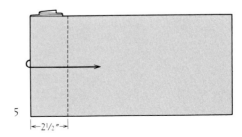

4–7. Turn paper over and fold as shown in each step.

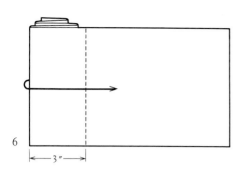

6

|← 3″ →|

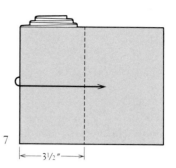

7

|← 3½″ →|

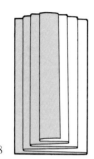

8

When entire paper is folded, light blue paper should be uppermost.

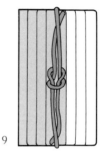

9

Write your message inside the card, then knot gold cord at center and tuck in ends.

46 Wedding Card

The overlapping folds of this matte gold and pearl white wedding card open to reveal a shikishi *bearing your message. The pale purity of the exterior colors is subtly complemented by the copper inside.*

MATERIALS
2 pieces 8½ × 4¼-inch copper paper
1 piece 8½ × 4¼-inch matte gold paper
1 piece 8½ × 4¼-inch pearl white paper
1 4⅛ × 4⅛-inch *shikishi* (see page 14)

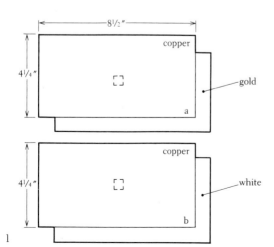

|← 8½″ →|

4¼″

copper

gold

a

copper

4¼″

white

b

1

Position copper paper and gold paper back to back, aligning corners, and fix in place with a small piece of double-face tape. Repeat with second sheet of copper paper and white paper.

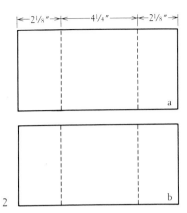

2

Score both sheets as shown.

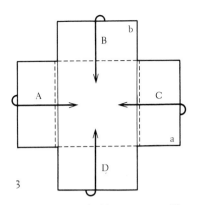

3

Lay the copper/gold set, copper side up, on the copper/white set, copper side up. Fix in place with a small piece of double-face tape. Fold flaps A and C, then B and D. Crease well.

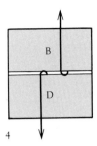

4

Unfold all four flaps.

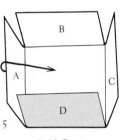

5

Fold flap A.

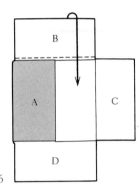

6

Fold flap B over A.

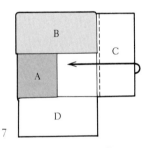

7

Fold flap C over B.

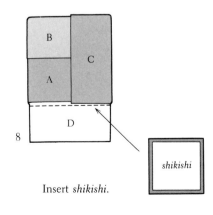

8

Insert *shikishi*.

shikishi

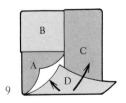

9

Fold flap D over C and tuck under A.

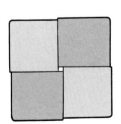

47 Wedding Card

This dignified card gives the impression of being made out of some precious metal. The glassine paper on top of the metallic copper looks light and tensile. A simple, brief message is most suitable.

MATERIALS

1 piece 12½ × 9-inch copper paper
1 piece 12 × 8½-inch white glassine paper
1 piece 11½ × 8-inch white glassine paper
gold cords

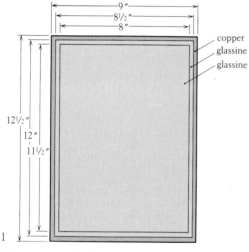

1 Center larger glassine paper on copper paper and carefully rub with a sheet of scrap paper to make them stick together. Center the smaller glassine paper on the larger one and repeat.

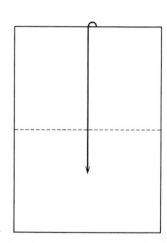

2 Turn the paper over and fold in half.

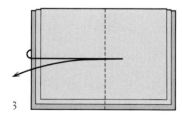

3 Fold the paper in half again, avoiding wrinkles at the top. Unfold.

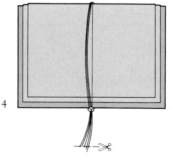

4 Wrap two gold cords together around the center and tie in a tight knot. Trim ends. Refold.

48 Wedding Card

The soft folds of this elegant card together with the matching cords produce an almost solemn impression. Press the creases firmly at the end, but gently in the middle to create fullness. The paper surface tends to show fingerprints, so use another sheet of paper or a ruler to press the folds. Write your message in gold ink, one line per panel.

MATERIALS
1 piece 19 × 6-inch matte gold paper
1 piece 18¼ × 5¼-inch champagne-color paper
gold cord

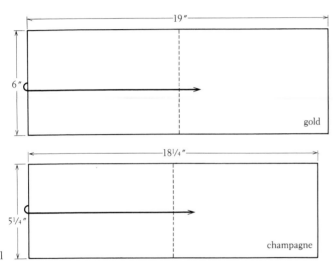

gold

champagne

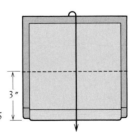

2

Center champagne-color paper on gold paper and fix in place with a small piece of double-face tape.

1

Fold both sheets in half.

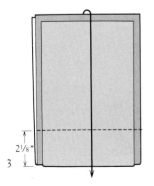

3

3–6 Fold as shown.

4

1¾"

3"

5

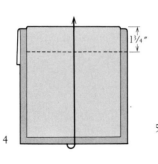

6

1⅞"

7

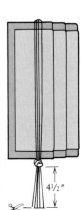

4½"

Write your message on one or more of the panels, then wrap a gold cord around the center and knot. Trim ends.

WHERE TO BUY JAPANESE PAPER

Japanese papers are available at large art-supply outlets, oriental import stores, and select stationery shops. Following is a representative listing.

AIKO'S ART MATERIALS IMPORT
714 North Wabash Avenue, Chicago, IL 60611
(312) 943–0745

AMSTERDAM ART
1013 University Avenue, Berkeley, CA 94710
(415) 548–9663

ANDREWS/NELSON/WHITEHEAD
31–10 48th Avenue, Long Island City, NY

BOOKS NIPPON
115 W. 57th Street, New York, NY 10019
(212) 582–4622

CANDO K. HOSHINO
1541 Clement Street, San Francisco, CA 94118
(415) 752–1636

KABUKI GIFTS AND IMPORTS
11355 Santa Monica Blvd., W. Los Angeles, CA 90025
(213) 477–2663

KAREL ART MATERIALS
737 Canal Street, Stamford, CT 06902
(203) 348–8996

KASURI DYEWORKS
1959 Shattuck Avenue, Berkeley, CA 94704
(415) 841–4509

KATE'S ART SUPPLY
2 W. 13th Street, New York, NY 10011
(212) 675–6406

KINOKUNIYA
1581 Webster Street, San Francisco, CA 94115
(415) 567–7625

LEE'S ART SHOP
220 W. 57th Street, New York, NY 10019
(212) 247–0110

NEW YORK CENTRAL ART SUPPLY
62 3rd Avenue, New York, NY 10003
(212) 473–7705

SAM FLAX
55 E. 55th Street, New York, NY 10022
(212) 620–3060

15 Park Row, New York, NY 10038
(212) 620–3030

25 E. 28th Street, New York, NY 10016
(212) 620–3040

747 3rd Avenue, New York, NY 10017
(212) 620–3050

12 W. 20th Street, New York, NY 10011
(212) 620–3038

ZEN ORIENTAL
521 5th Avenue, New York, NY 10017
(212) 697–0840

115 W. 57th Street, New York, NY 10019
(212) 582–4622